The Shrewd Christian

You Can't Have It All, But You Can Have **More Than Enough**

Neil Atkinson

WATERBROOK
PRESS

THE SHREWD CHRISTIAN
PUBLISHED BY WATERBROOK PRESS
2375 Telstar Drive, Suite 160
Colorado Springs, Colorado 80920
A division of Random House, Inc.

ISBN 1-57856-796-3

Library of Congress Cataloging-in-Publication Data
Atkinson, Neil.
    The shrewd Christian : you can't have it all, but you can have more than enough / Neil Atkinson.—1st ed.
       p. cm.
    ISBN 1-57856-796-3
    1. Wealth—Religious aspects—Christianity. 2. Finance, Personal—Religious aspects—Christianity. I. Title.
BR115 .W4A75 2004
241'.68—dc22   2003021611

Printed in the United States of America
2004

10 9 8 7 6 5 4 3

Praise for
The Shrewd Christian

"Neil Atkinson has an extremely solid biblical perspective on personal finances. As he states, 'Shrewd Christians do not *ignore* money or *stop* at money. They go *through* money and get *past* money so they can be involved in more important things.' I highly recommend this book. It's fun, serious, and full of practical helps."

—DENNY RYDBERG, president of Young Life, an international
outreach ministry to adolescents

"What I love about this book is the coupling of callings: that people matter and money matters. *The Shrewd Christian* is a fantastic guide to improving your economy while maintaining your people-are-primary philosophy."

—MARILYN MEBERG, author of *The Zippered Heart* and speaker
for the Women of Faith conferences

"Neil Atkinson does a masterful job of offering the 'Christian Middle Class' practical solutions to everyday financial issues. *The Shrewd Christian* challenges and encourages God's people to live as biblically wise stewards in an increasingly hostile world."

—DAVID BRIGGS, director of the Good Sense Stewardship
Ministry at Willow Creek Community Church

"Neil's wry sense of humor punctuates each page of *The Shrewd Christian;* his years of personal experience and his wisdom make this book invaluable. *The Shrewd Christian* makes it not only possible but simple and fun to control money instead of letting it control you."

—GRACE KETTERMAN, child and family psychiatrist, and author
of numerous books, including *When You Feel Like Screaming*

"Neil helps us understand how we can reach the goals of gladness and contentment and how costly it is to our souls when we allow finances to be the center of our affections. As you read Neil's wise counsel in this book, you will hear the voice of Jesus whispering in your ear, 'Follow me.' Neil encourages and teaches us to stop listening to the 'Bad Shepherds' in our society and to keep our souls aligned with the Good Shepherd, Jesus."

—CRAIG WILLIFORD, PhD, president of Denver Seminary

This book is dedicated to Margie—our eternal marriage argument continues. But in this book I get the last word: You are, and always have been, The Best!

And to our children Matt and Jodi.
Matt, I should have bought you the second doughnut at Meier Thrifty Acres. Jodi, I should not have sent you to first grade with the duct-taped luggage handle attached to your lunch box.

Special Thanks

*I would like to give special thanks to William Raymond Atkinson I
and Erma Edna Edith Stick Atkinson—They could have taught the
most frugal person in the world a thing or two.*

*To Edith Meberg for inspiring me by example
to understand that no one ever gets old. Ever.*

And to Sverre Meberg, the best father-in-law I ever had.

To the WaterBrook team: A rookie author is grateful for your guidance.

*To Steve Cobb for believing in the project and Elisa Fryling Stanford for
proving that a young pup can teach an old dog new things.*

Contents

Part One: A Middle-Class Revolution
(You didn't skip the introduction, did you?)

What does it mean to be shrewd? Are you Financially Alert or Financially Comatose? Here we will look at how money and Jesus compete and why Jesus tells us to be sheep among wolves. I will also tell you about the financial wastelands my family went through, and why Shrewd Christians do not ignore money.

In a retold parable, we will see that Jesus did not commend dishonesty, but he did commend shrewdness. The purpose of money is to build relationships; to realize this purpose, we have to know who our master is.

What are the counterfeits of shrewd, and why will they keep you from becoming wealthy? How are the Gang of Three brainwashing you? Here we'll look at why you need to be your own financial consultant, and what Table Manners you need to get there.

Learn the key question to ask yourself on the way to True Riches. Look at the difference between wealth and a lifestyle of wealth, and discover why you can live like most millionaires.

What does it mean to be truly rich? Learn why money is not the source of problems in marriage, and how you can be on the same page with your spouse.

PART TWO: MAKING IT WORK

I am sending you out like sheep among wolves. Therefore be as shrewd as snakes and as innocent as doves.

—MATTHEW 10:16

Be on your guard against all kinds of greed; a man's life does not consist in the abundance of his possessions.

—LUKE 12:15

Do Not Skip This Part!

This book is for the Christian Middle Class. I am one of you. We need this book.

Most financial books are about money. This one is about life. Don't worry, it will deal with money. But life must come first.

About 75 percent of people in the United States are considered "middle class." Twenty percent are considered working class or poor, and 5 percent rich. The poor and the rich have other books to help them. This one is for you and me.

The term *middle class* is too broad to be narrowly defined by money. The terms *white collar* and *blue collar* are not only outdated, but they have no correlation with the amount of one's income. (A cardiologist had a plumbing problem. The plumber fixed the problem in three minutes and presented a bill for $75. The astonished doctor said, "I am a heart specialist, and I don't charge that much for my services." The plumber smiled and replied, "Neither did I when I was a cardiologist.")

Occupation, education, and lifestyle are indicators of this segment of our society. Apparel, experience, even neighborhoods broadly define this phenomenon. Therefore, for the purpose of this book, if you feel you are middle class, you are.

Many of the Christian Middle Class (CMC) are in Trouble—with a capital *T*. Financial trouble is the *root cause* of other troubles: worry, guilt, stress, lack of freedom. It is also a *symptom* of other root causes: an impaired relationship with God, your spouse, your kids, and yourself.

Most financial books assume we are "economic people" who must handle money as an entity outside ourselves. But our *person* (*ish* in Hebrew) is dependent on relationships for life. People are primary; money is secondary. Therefore, money must be seen in the context of relationships and how it can enable our relationships to grow.

This book is written for normal people by a normal person. (Do not ask me to prove the last part of that statement.) I am assuming that you are a normal middle-class Christian. You are in a class with those who feel they never have enough money and can barely keep their financial noses above water. You would like to give more, or even something, to the Lord, but things are tight, and guilt mounts.

This book is about *your* economy. It is not about *the* economy. I am not concerned about helping rich people. I care about you: hard-working, hard-pressed, battle-fatigued men and women who deserve more than their current situations are giving them.

The following pages could change your life. They could help you grow. They could make you think. The least they will do is entertain you. Here are a few specific things I hope this book will do for you:

- It will help you become the person you are meant to be. In all likelihood, you picked up this book to get help with money issues. It is just as likely that because of our culture's insidious, poisoned view of finances you have become a facsimile, in some ways, of the real you. In other words, the world in which you live has subtly and continually repatterned your mind and squeezed you into its mold. This book will remind you of who you are free to be.
- It will help you find time in your life to become an economic force.
- It will help you maximize your time to develop a money game plan that will bring laughter back into the lives of you and your family.
- It will help you become truly rich and financially wealthy.

Big talk. If you feel "stuck" financially, you are hoping that this book will back up that talk, and I think it will. Welcome to the revolution.

Surprised by Financial Wealth

My wife, Margie, and I were surprised to find out a few years ago that a mutual fund retirement survey ranked us in the top 8 percent of the country in terms of monetary wealth. We were wealthy! We were not just surprised—we were stunned! Why?

- We've gone through times of living on a very small salary.
- Investments were not always kind to us.
- We have never had a windfall inheritance.
- We have made a number of dumb (and worse) mistakes.
- We have never actually pursued wealth.

Margie and I had known that we were truly rich because of Jesus. What we didn't know was that we were financially wealthy. Though we (read: I) made some wondrous blunders (a *blunder* is way beyond a mistake, and a *wondrous blunder* is way beyond a common old blunder), we had come out on top—not rich, but wealthy. Somewhere along the line we started thinking about money in a new way, and that began a revolution in our home.

What is this new way of thinking? Am I pointing you to armed resistance or rural "off-the-grid" independence or a vow of poverty? Not a chance. No, the best move for the CMC is to develop an intentional lifestyle that will lead to both true riches and financial wealth. Here's the key: More life, less money. (Can't you just see the TV ad? One person yelling, "More life!" The other shouting back, "Less money!") The down-and-dirty of how to have more life for less money is in learning how to go to war and win, how to get in the game and win.

You didn't know you were fighting in a financial war? You are. You didn't know you were playing a financial game? You are. If you aren't aware of those facts, you are bound to lose. And you can't *afford* to lose. The war is called Consumer Economy. That means, simply, that the vast majority of goods and services exist to meet the supposed needs of individuals. This is serious stuff. Our adversaries in the financial war are very professional. They play for keeps. This is their battle plan:

- Discover people's deepest needs.
- Determine their media habits (television, radio, magazines, movies, newspapers, for example).
- Tailor a package for their niche.
- Offer too many choices with a sense of urgency.
- *Confuse* them.
- Leave them with the message that they will not be whole without *this* product.
- Start over.
- Keep going.
- Faster.
- Way faster.

The Consumer Economy wins. The CMC loses. The revolution starts the moment we understand what is happening to us and how we can intentionally engage in the action and win. We win when we pay attention to these revolution formulas:

$$TR + KoRR = L$$
True Riches plus the Kingdom of Right Relationships equals Life.

$$LT + E(T) + A^2 = L$$
Little Things done Excellently over Time and Applied Appropriately add up to Lots!

There it is. Piece of pizza.

Notice that the formula is not:

$$1BT + P(I) = L$$

One Big Thing (as in the lottery, an inheritance, a ground-floor business, and so on) done Perfectly and Immediately leads to Lots.

That formula will only move us toward *less*. We must not play the game perfectly; only excellently.

My experience as a perfectionist, and with near-perfectionists, indicates that we get discouraged by setbacks and stop fighting after a few surprises appear. I learned the hard way. I failed at certain things. You will learn about those things as you read this book. You need to understand how and why I failed so you can buy into excellence, not perfection.

Knowing the little things and how they work together will give us freedom. This book will provide information—and accurate information stops confusion in its tracks. Truth helps us sort out the dangers we face, helps us recognize the enemy without and within, and helps us focus on a realistic, holistic strategy so we can join the revolution.

We need to recognize reality: Denial is *not* a river in Egypt. Delusion will not make things better. We must think about money in a new way.

TRUE RICHES AND FINANCIAL WELL-BEING

Part of the middle-class revolution I'm proposing involves countering the lies that are fed to us on a daily basis—lies that put your financial foundation on a bed of sand, such as:

1. It is completely your fault that you are in credit-card debt.
2. Recessions happen because you do not spend enough.
3. Safety is risky.
4. You need more stuff to be happy.

Lies. The other side is not playing fair. When our human nature collides with the culture, we can easily enter a financial lock-up. We want the Get-Out-of-Jail-Free card. We want freedom.

While this book could help you become financially wealthy, that is just part of the goal. And a minor part at that! Our destination is to become truly rich *and* financially wealthy. It is possible to achieve that status without lapsing into the errors of the Prosperity Gospel or get-rich-now idiocies. The freedom we're after will enrich every part of our lives.

Ultimately, this book is about generosity. God's generosity has led us to true riches. Our generosity keeps us in true riches. Generosity can mean giving money or not giving money—whichever is, in reality, more generous. Generosity can also mean sending messages of affection, encouragement, attention, and laughter. Generosity has a little to do with money, and a lot to do with life—especially with how we develop successful relationships.

We will raise our standard of living when we raise our standard of giving. We can be generous to all people when we understand that we have been treated generously. We can be generous with our money when we have money. If we are financially rich, we may be generous or we may appear to be generous. Often, it is the latter. Appearances are the games we play in front of humans. Reality is what we live before God. And the heart of God is generosity.

We may well be growing, exciting Christians—or not. It does not matter. We are fortunate that God accepts the nongenerous, the whiners, the vindictive, and the ungrateful as well as the proud and the arrogant into His world. He does so with the idea of re-creating us. He is continually hounding us to move from that familiar country of selfishness toward the state of generosity whose capital is contentment.

Admittedly, the ideas in this book are radical. You can *improve* your life by adopting a few of the book's mechanisms in one sector of life. You can change your life by looking at the effect money has on every part of your life, including discipleship. You are entering a freeway that leads to riches and financial wealth. It will have a very positive impact on your life, but this is not a weekend jaunt. This highway must be traveled and applied over time. It will take you about nine months to arrive at this new life. But you will see results in seven days and feel the positive impact in thirty days.

The Change Artist

The average Christian is an excellent actor. We just end up that way. Notice that people leaving a church service are almost all smiling and friendly. What could be a greater witness for the Lord than happy families attending Sunday services? Everything is fine with everyone, thank you very much.

Haven't we all been stunned to learn that Christians we know and love are filing for divorce? We had no clue anything was wrong. Good actors. And yet marriage difficulty is not the Number One Conversational No-No among Christians. Money is. How much you earn. How you spend it. What you think about it.

Talking about money would be impolite. Oh sure, we hear some sermonly platitudes about tithing every year at "Commitment Sunday": "God loves a cheerful giver." "You can't *out-give* God!" We all go away feeling guilty about letting the Lord down and vowing to do better next year. But what about down-to-earth, practical, realistic, honest talking about money? We don't talk about that until it's too late. We go off perfecting our art of performance and hoping that some day we will get things under control in our financial lives.

Today is the day of your salvation from the evil master called money. We can change. We "normal" middle-class Christians can alter the way we live and increase the quality of our lives. Believers have so much going for them that it is *never* too late; resurrection is possible in every life situation.

We cannot stop our lives to work on finances any more than we can stop our lives to fix our broken spiritual or physical parts. We have to work on things while life is progressing and every part of our lives must be involved in this exercise, *in toto.* We do not have the luxury of separating out one segment of our lives, putting it on a workbench and fixing it.

In the next chapters we will deal with how you can become a change artist. How you can move from living in denial and delusion to becoming spiritually healthy and financially responsible. You will also become financially wealthy, but not at the expense of your spiritual health. The two must go together.

Let me repeat: This book is about living life and developing financial wealth. Notice the order: life and then money. We can have life. We can have money. Some of us will have one or the other. Some of us will have both. I will guarantee one thing: If you have money but not life, you have nothing. Life is not the result of money.

Our travels in this book will take us down a strange road for a spiritual journey. But it is Interstate 1. Radical discipleship does not occur until we master this monster. And we have no choice—as we'll see, Jesus did not allow for a "pass" on the money question.

A revolution is waiting to happen in your finances. Your goal is to blow by mediocrity and arrive at Financial Excellence. But the greater revolution is waiting to happen in your life. Money will guide you to freedom and generosity. Strange, but true.

Onward.

Part
One

A Middle-Class Revolution

(You Didn't Skip the Introduction, Did You?)

The Reason for Shrewd

The Shrewd Christian." An intriguing phrase, a novel description. On the one hand, the idea is appealing. On the other hand, something doesn't seem quite right. In the context of finances, *shrewd* might imply using quasi-ethical procedures to distort scriptural imperatives. Nothing is further from the truth.

Webster clears up the confusion in his little book. According to him, the word *shrewd* has two conflicting definitions: (1) "mischievous, wicked, bad;" and (2) "[exercising or having] far-sighted judgment, astute in practical matters, [keen] of mind."

If we apply the first definition to the phrase "Shrewd Christian," Christians will, correctly, recoil in horror. If we apply the second definition, most non-Christians will fall over laughing. In our culture, *shrewdness* and *Christian* do not go together.

Many intellectuals and corporate gurus see us as nice, gullible, unsophisticated, and simple—anything but shrewd. Ted Turner, the communications mogul, put it bluntly: "Christianity is for losers." They might describe Christians euphemistically: "Their tank is not quite full" or "They are not the sharpest knives in the drawer." My favorite phrase I heard at Starbucks is "They do not row with both oars in the water." People with only one oar in the water go around in circles with no hope of arriving at their goal—unless, of course, their goal is to become dizzy.

In truth, rowing with one oar *is* a fitting metaphor for much of the Christian Middle Class (CMC). Christians should be heading straight for their financial goals using both oars, but we often use only one oar and end up financially dizzy, going nowhere fast. Outside forces combine with our internal nature to move us toward a whirlpool that will suck us under. Our lives, our families, and our discipleship are threatened. We become lawful prey to those who know that we are going around in circles.

In order to become *shrewd*—far-sighted, astute, pragmatic, and wary— we need to know where we are now. Every individual, couple, or family fits into one of the following four categories:

1. *The Financially Alert.* "We always desire to learn, understand, and practice insights from other people. We are living in financial security." These people are *Financially Confident.* They have, essentially, mastered money and are living more life on less money. But they always like to pick up ideas.

2. *The Financially Aware.* "We are doing okay, but know we could do better. We have a vague sense of unease about our finances." These people are *Financially Nervous.* They are aware of what is going on in their finances, but sometimes money seems to be closing in on them.

3. *The Financially Conscious.* "We are not quite making ends meet—we acquired a 'consolidation loan' to get out of this 'one-time' difficult circumstance! We have a serious sense of financial unease." These people are *Financially Troubled.* They are not quite making ends meet, and they're beginning to lose hope. Money has, essentially, mastered them.

4. *The Financially Comatose.* "We have a large amount of credit-card debt. We are just making the minimum monthly payments and have lost hope. We are past unease and into panic." These people are *Financially Claustrophobic.* Money has captured every aspect of their lives. Creditors call at any time and any place. Living in denial and delusion, they hope Jesus will come soon.

Living in one of the four categories is due *mostly* to our own efforts. But these categories are not static; we can progress or regress to another category at any time. Regression to a more precarious category occurs not only because of our own efforts but also because of outside "help" from our culture.

You can see the effects of our culture's strategies on our finances if you look at where we are now: Tremendous economic expansion has taken place in the last decade or so, but somehow it missed most of us. Somehow the Christian Middle Class, the backbone of America, has seen unsecured debt rise to dangerous levels; work hours, bankruptcies, and foreclosures increase; and real wages decrease. Then the recession hit. But good news from the economists! This downturn was relatively quick and painless. Unless you were one of the people knocked silly through a job loss or portfolio "adjustment" or made the mistake of being employed by a company that unexpectedly disappeared. Unless you were one of the thousands of retired people trudging back to the work force! Quick? Painless? On which planet are those economists living? But all is not lost! The well-to-do are better off. Doesn't that bring a smile to your soul?

Money was meant to serve us. We are not working "for money," nor should we be serving money; yet most of the CMC are working for and serving money. (An easy reality test: Do you have credit-card debt that is not related to health issues, an accident, or a disaster? If your answer is yes, congratulations, you are in the majority of America's middle class who are money servants.)

Regardless of how the middle class got into the mess we're in, we will only get out of it on our own. The ones who helped push us into difficulty will not help us out of our difficulty. They are glad we are there; it helps their bottom line.

Of the four groups of people just mentioned, only one has the chance to become wealthy: the Financially Alert. Each of the other three groups is operating on a very narrow financial margin. They are endangering themselves and their families, possibly without knowing it.

Let's look more closely at this idea of *margin*. We live in Colorado

Springs. Pikes Peak is our neighbor. In the summer, cars can drive up the mountain to the summit. The view is magnificent, the dropoff severe and deadly. (There's an old saying around here about the Pikes Peak dropoff: "It is not the fall that will hurt you, it is the sudden stop at the end.") Picture yourself and your family driving to the top of the mountain. How much room would you want between your right wheels and the edge of that road?

Your passengers' advice would be to keep that margin of safety as wide as possible. Stay toward the center as long as possible. A wide margin of safety will protect you from unanticipated events like an animal jumping in front of the car, a rock rolling downhill, a gust of wind, or inattention. It would strike most of us as foolhardy, dumb, immature, or negligent to drive with a portion of the right front wheel hanging off the edge of the road.

Yet many Christians are living with a very narrow financial margin; they are living with a wheel hanging off the financial highway. They are, in reality, one paycheck away from disaster. How long could they live without income? Any unplanned event—job loss, furnace breakdown, children's surgery, parents needing help—would crumple their world. That condition is dangerous, not shrewd.

Our great adventure involves making steady progress to reach financial confidence with the greatest amount of margin and staying there. The adventure is easy to understand, easy to execute and easy to achieve. Simply put: Over the next year you will learn to have more life and spend less money. Do I need to repeat that? If you have more life on less money, you will be on your way to becoming financially wealthy.

As the middle class, we are not rich, and we will probably never be rich. Rich means having anything you want, anytime you want it, without looking at the price. (If you just mumbled to yourselves, "Must be nice," you are in deep weeds, and this book will really, really help you.) Financially wealthy means that at a certain age you have developed an appropriate amount of wealth. You have put basic financial practices into place and are financially free. You do not have it all, but you have more than enough—for the rest of your life. Here are the seven characteristics that describe the truly rich and financially wealthy:

1. You are becoming a generous person in all aspects of life. A mundane example of this is doing something at home that needs doing even though it is your spouse's responsibility.
2. You are being generous with your money.
3. Your home is paid off.
4. Your kids' educations are funded.
5. You have no debt.
6. You live an appropriate lifestyle (i.e., "more than enough").
7. You have a pool of conservatively invested money from which living expenses could be drawn five years past your estimated age of death (men: seventy-six; women: eighty-one).

Shrewd Christians do not *ignore* money, nor do they *stop* at money. They go *through* money and get *past* money so they can be involved in more important things.

Do you want to have a life, or do you want to pretend to have a life? The first is real. The second is a mirage that depends on competition, comparison, appearance, and assumption. Money is in the way. We can't deny it or go around it. We need to go through it to get to freedom.

THE CHIEF COMPETITION OF JESUS

Money is important to God because money is the chief competition of Jesus. In other words, money can lead us away from God. We will either serve money or we will serve Jesus. Therefore, we do not focus on wealth just for the sake of being wealthy. Money does not determine our significance. But the *use* of money is intrinsically tied into discipleship. The correct handling of money is critical to living a full life.

It seems paradoxical, if not odd, that we can increase our connection with Jesus by traveling the money road. But Jesus was very interested in money. It disturbed Him that He had to compete with it for people's hearts. But He gave us choices. Following His choices leads to life—life far more abundant than we have imagined. As life expands, we thrive. Sometimes we thrive in the worst of circumstances. Not following His choices leads to mere existence. Life diminishes, we survive. Sometimes we are just surviving even though we are in the best of circumstances.

The idea of using spiritual principles to move from financial la-la land to financial wealth may go against your long-held understandings. Let's reverse that thinking and see if it helps: The world/business culture around you is using nonspiritual principles to move you from financial wealth into financial la-la land. There, is that better?

Jesus' goal was to revolutionize the world. He wanted the world to be transformed. His strategy was love. His death and resurrection reflected a sacrifice and power that would enable us to become new persons—in every way. Jesus did not compartmentalize life. He came to save our lives in their entirety. That means not only our spiritual lives but our financial and relational lives as well, because they relate to who we are.

Nearly half of the parables of Jesus have to do with money. Money is the subject of more than two thousand verses in the Bible—more than the verses on love and faith combined. This doesn't mean that either the rich or the poor have more of God's favor than the CMC. Many rich believe that they have earned a life of entitlement. The Bible would not agree with that misconception. Many poor believe that they are owed a life of entitlement. God does have a special concern for the poor, but "entitlement" smacks of self-centeredness. Once again, we would find the Bible disagreeing with that misconception.

Jesus told his disciples, "I am sending you out like sheep among wolves. Therefore be as shrewd as snakes and as innocent as doves" (Matthew 10:16). I am not sure that was a comforting comment to those who heard His words. Send out sheep among the wolves? If you and I had been in the audience when He mentioned the sheep and wolves thing, we probably would have turned to one another for clarification.

"Did He say what I thought He said: We should be the sheep, and our job is to be out among the wolves?"

"No, that can't be right. We must have misunderstood."

"It goes against our very nature!"

"As near as I can understand, sheep have teeth suited for chewing, and wolves, which are larger to begin with, have teeth suited for devouring."

"Do you know what a wolf calls a sheep that is innocent but not shrewd? Lunch! That couldn't be what Jesus is saying."

But that is exactly what Jesus expects from those who follow Him. It is a radical idea. But He knew He would not be sending us alone; He would be with us. (The odds, therefore, are in our favor.) And He gave us a practice to follow that would keep us safe. That practice has two parts—two oars, if you will. We need to be *shrewd as snakes* and *innocent as doves.* These two things work in tandem. If the oar of shrewdness is given equal power with the oar of innocence, we will be on a straight course to freedom.

The majority of middle-class Christians have mastered the second half of that equation. We are innocent as doves; we are financially naive. We are also hard-working, bright people. We are people of faith. We are trusting people. We even trust the wolves disguised as people—over and over again. We have not mastered the first half of the equation: shrewd as snakes.

As people explain their financial problems, I often hear phrases like: "We didn't spend on anything big or inappropriate," "It's not as if we went crazy or anything like that," "It was the surprise of the third child [or insert the reason of your choice] that did us in." "Look, we clip coupons and turn out the lights when we leave a room. Nothing is helping."

When I hear this kind of thing I ask, "Have you really tried *everything?*"

"Yes."

"Literally, *everything?*"

A more frustrated, "YES! Weren't you listening?"

"Then you have intentionally lowered your standard of living?"

"What do you mean by 'lowered your standard of living'?"

"You've sold your second car or home, spend zero dollars, and refrain from visiting shopping malls? That sort of thing."

Their look is not the glazed look of a deer staring at the headlights of a car. It is more like a deer's eyes as it realizes it is about to enter deer heaven; a mixture of fear, panic, anger, and resignation. They are about to get creamed. Or they think I have lost my mind. The very idea of retreating is completely foreign to them. Their current lifestyle is their preordained right. They are sure their thinking is biblical. They want to know: If God is real, why isn't He bailing them out?

Apart from medical problems, accidents, or disasters, *most financial trouble is the result of small, incremental lifestyle choices that have caused Financial Claustrophobia.* People have been set up by the money game, have very innocently bought into the game, and have been ensnared. They are doing "everything" they can, but it is not working. They look at me as if they want me to say, "Golly, you are right. You are the only ones in the world in your situation. You are really stuck. Here is $10,000. That is the only way out. Thank you for letting me help."

I do not say that.

We must develop a sense of appropriate toughness, wisdom, and street smarts to navigate the money trap; we need to become shrewd. Our society has led us to believe that we cannot do this without the help of "experts," people who know how to handle money. We have learned that we cannot trust ourselves. That's nonsense; we are the only ones we should trust with our money—that is, after we have attained shrewdness.

It's time to become Shrewd Christians as well as innocent Christians. Shrewd Christians do not love money; they use money as a tool to have a more abundant life of discipleship.

Through the Wastelands

Are Margie and I Shrewd Christians who have mastered money and developed wealth? Yes. Are we Shrewd Christians who have all the answers and never make financial mistakes? No. (The mere thought of that question is laughable!) Are we Shrewd Christians because our background is wealth or because we have been trained as accountants or financial planners? No.

We are middle-class people who have experienced the realities of life. We did not inherit our wealth or even make geographic moves that brought dramatic house appreciation. We did have a very good financial education. We earned our Masters in Finance from the School of Hard Knocks—the school colors are black and blue. (The alma mater was, "I've been cheated, been mistreated; when will I wise up?") We made way too many errors in our early years. Naiveté gave way to pride, and eventually pride gave way to shrewdness, so we could master money and gain true riches.

Let me start near the beginning. Early in our marriage we lived on a very small salary; we had to go up a notch to hit poverty level. I managed our finances. We were idealists. But we had been raised as solid middle-class people. If a soap opera had been named after me at this stage of life, it would have been called *The Young and the Naive*.

The ministry organization I served put all new staff through a comprehensive testing program. One of the tests was for economic motivation. According to that test, my initial ranking (in terms of the likelihood of becoming rich) was in the lower one percent of the country. That means out of one hundred people, I was the only one not motivated by money. How low was our pay? For the first fourteen years of our ministry, our salary was capped at whatever a first-year teacher made in that district. It didn't matter if we were married with children, had advanced degrees, whatever. That was our salary. Every year we made what the new batch of teachers made. My organization saw to it that we stayed in that category.

(Someone once asked our supervisor why salaries were so low. The reply was a classic: "They are low to keep out the riffraff.") After fourteen years our salaries rose to match those of a teacher with the same amount of experience and education. We were stunned with this increase. We were also stunned to find that our expenses rose to meet this new income.

Our family lived in a nice house, courtesy of the Lord. He saw to it that we did not get a salary from our ministry organization for seven months when we were first married. What a gift! Margie and I had to improvise like crazy, using her substitute teacher earnings to help cover living expenses. But we were in love and committed to doing the ministry together. What fun! At the end of the seven months, we received *all* of our back pay. That was the down payment on our first home. I am sure I would have found ways to spend that money if we had received a check every month.

It was hard to live and minister in affluent areas without being affected by the neighborhood. I had always liked nice things, and as I grew older, I longed for the "finer" things of life. But, of course, we couldn't afford them. (Are you smelling trouble here? Your sniffer is correct.) There had to be a way that we could have it all. There was a way. I became interested in investing. I became quite good at it. I made a large amount of money in stocks, bonds, and commodity trading. I was very proud of what I had accomplished financially. If a soap opera had been named after me during this stage of life, it would have been called *The Proud and the Arrogant*.

The Lord has a unique punishment for the Proud and the Arrogant: He allows them to remain in that condition. He knew the pattern that would evolve. Pride would pay me; the wage would be financial death.

Here is how it happened: After reaping the financial bonanza (more than I had made in eighteen months of salary), I chatted with the beautiful people. I listened to their advice. They somberly listened, nodded, and said, "Tax shelter." I somberly listened, nodded, and said to myself, "Hey, ain't I something?" It was heady stuff realizing that I, as a low-paid minister, needed a tax shelter. Whooee! I was good! (For those of you who smelled trouble earlier, you now sense an odor that can only be described as "stink.")

But I did have my principles! I was not going to trust non-Christians with my money. I was much too smart for that. I sought help from a Christian brother. ("Mr. Sheep, I would like you to meet Mr. Wolf.") He would surely tell me the best and safest way to invest my profits to shelter the gains. He would give me the best advice. Certainly he wouldn't take advantage of a poor little minister. (Sing it with me: "Na-Na Nah, Nah...")

This financial advisor lauded me for my financial achievements. He said it was inconceivable that I had done so well on my limited income. He had never seen anything like it. Funny thing, Margie was not all that impressed with my financial acumen or with this expert. She was reserved and thoughtful. I did not consult her—after all, I was a financial guru.

You could have predicted the result. ("My, my, Mr. Sheep, you look a little bewildered. You have been sheared.") I lost every dime I had made, and three years later the IRS denied the tax shelter. I did not even protest; I just forked over the $4,000. If a soap opera had been named after me during this stage of life, it would have been called *The Crumbled and the Humbled*.

From that time forward, I became my own investment counselor. I chucked the advice of the "beautiful people" and did my own thing. I had learned an expensive lesson, but I developed a sound investment strategy out of it. That strategy is based on two premises: (1) I would never again invest in something I did not fully understand; and (2) I would never again ignore the eyes of my wife. If she is in doubt about anything, I take note. (She is *probably* wrong because I am so smart. Yet there is that slight possibility...)

These principles became our investment guidelines—easily understood, very simple to practice, and, as it turned out, very profitable. When relatives, friends, neighbors, or stockbrokers (a.k.a. "sales machines"!)

arrived at my door with an idea, I just told them I did not fully under-stand their product and I would get back to them after I did my research. I seldom followed through. When I did, I was glad I had not invested in that product.

So we began to become wealthy through accumulation, not invest-ments. In time we moved from an idealistic view (how life *should* work) to a more pragmatic view (how life *does* work).

I hope you get a chance to meet Margie someday. One of the reasons I know that God is good is that He pointed me to her. She is analytical, academic, and the only person in the world who could have made Mother Teresa look mean. She is also intensely competitive. She is nicer than I am, so she can mask her competitiveness. But together we form a great team. Consequently, we took our low pay as a personal challenge. Take the sub-ject of family food. I call it the Margie Way to Wealth.

Margie shopped well and planned well. Her plan was very detailed. One Saturday afternoon I grabbed an apple from the refrigerator and began to eat it. Margie walked into the kitchen, saw the apple disappearing, and with a look of dismay said, "That apple was salad for Thursday." Oops.

The great gift of having a little money is that when you learn to thrive on a little, you can do extremely well on a little more. We found ways to create a little more. Everything was judged in terms of savings, value, and productivity. Everything! We left nothing to chance. We had *no* margin for error. My economic naiveté was left in the dust.

Time marched on. (It has a way of doing that.) We were within three years of paying off our home and our cottage in Michigan when the Lord called us to another location. It was much more expensive to live in Over-land Park than in Grand Rapids. How could we possibly adjust to this expensive community—especially on our salary? But we moved and adjusted.

More years went by and the kids got set for college. They wanted to attend a private school. Hmm, I still have a low salary. But oh, I forgot, we had our house paid off two months before our daughter, Jodi, started at Baylor. We could just transfer the house payment to the college payment. Total college debt for eight years of schooling (two kids times four years): $2,700, which included the cost of a mission trip that Jodi wanted to do after her senior year. We had not planned on that additional expense. But we were able to pull it off.

So the house was paid off, college was finished, our son, Matt, had married Kellie, and Jodi was doing well on her own. We had no debt of any kind. But as the years passed and our income increased, we regressed and let the pace of life dictate our spending habits. Then... "What's that, Lord? Excuse me, did I hear correctly? You want us to move to Colorado Springs, and you have a job for Margie? And you want me to retire for a time? But Lord, that would result in moving to a more expensive city *and* reducing our income by 33 percent! Yes, Lord, I know my work here is finished. I did what You asked me to do, but Lord, we have friends, a church, and, well, to be truthful, I am getting on in years and this is a good financial situation. What? Okay, I will start packing!"

Off we went with one-third less income to an area that was 50 percent more expensive. We were back to the financial mess of having a home mortgage—the biggest one ever. Margie was now the main breadwinner. Talk about being turned upside down and inside out.

We were now in financial warm water. But the Lord indicated that this was the right move for us. We could not take His call seriously and let a little thing like money stand in the way. Very quickly I moved back into what we had discovered in our idyllic years in Grand Rapids. I shopped with an attitude, remembering the Margie Way to Wealth. I applied this plan to all the financial aspects of our life.

Meanwhile, Margie hit on all cylinders in her new job and within two years was promoted to vice president. I golfed, skied, oversaw the completion of our new home, put a financial system into place, and got very, very bored. I had loved my job and the outfit for which I had worked.

I started a leadership foundation, discovered a marvelous tool called the IDAK Career Match, and switched to career consulting. I opened a business and bought every piece of equipment with cash. Stayed out of debt. Scary at first, and then it got worse. Somehow the business became profitable.

Money, as always in our marriage, was a nonissue. We couldn't have it all, but we had more than enough. When we wanted to join a very nice, private club, we did it. When we wanted another vehicle, a painting, furniture, or a trip, we did it. When Margie needed new clothes, she bought them. We helped our children financially from time to time. We found countless ways to give money away to organizations and to individuals. And again, time was marching on, slowly but surely. So slowly and so surely that I did not recognize what was happening, although I was a little concerned about our spending.

Then we got to the point of needing a new will. (By the way, you do have a will, don't you?) We had to follow a few procedures. We had to make out a financial statement. In doing so I began to calculate the sum of money we would need to set aside so that we would be financially free—a reservoir of money that would carry us through our final years. I knew we had a long way to go before we were free.

It was an exercise in diligence to prepare the statement: gathering the records, adding assets and subtracting liabilities, and making the other internal accounting adjustments. The result was shocking. There must be something wrong. I panicked. What had I messed up? I redid the figures. I called Margie in. We redid the figures. Figures do not lie! We had become wealthy. The numbers indicated that we could live at our current standard of living (without Social Security) for twenty-five years, until we are both well into our golden years. And then, if necessary, we could sell the house. That would bring in a few more bucks. We could retire now if we desired. We chose to celebrate. We went out for a Baskin-Robbins ice cream cone. Paid cash. Life was good!

Now there are three assumptions involved in the above scenario:

1. We will be able to keep our health;
2. Our children and grandchildren will continue to be healthy; and
3. We will not be involved in a terrible accident or disaster.

As I looked at those numbers I thought, *How could this be?* I had crushed our family by being prideful. We became very conservative in our investments. We even missed the bull market! We shouldn't be wealthy. Look at what the financial people were saying. We hadn't listened. So how could we be very well off? But we, as an average middle-class couple, became financially wealthy.

It gets better. On September 12, 2001, I started playing the financial game with a new goal. The goal was to live very well on less than half of the money we made. We are winning the game. Don't take my word for it, take Margie's: "Neil has many good ideas. And some ideas that are not so good. I was skeptical of the approach to live on less money. But I am a competitive person. It sounded like lentils, yogurt, and no heat in the house. And it turned out it was lentils, yogurt, and no heat in the house. But we made it fun. Neil made sure that he took a lot of the home responsibility off of my shoulders. He became even more creative in his cooking, and I am a sucker for good food. We did not become hermits; we just enjoyed life more on less money."

I wish I could say that Margie and I were always Shrewd Christians regarding money. But I can't say that. However, 2 Corinthians 1:3-8 gives an idea of why the Lord let us go through the financial wasteland before we got to the financial promised land. We had to become radical to survive and then to thrive. This is a strategy for you, the Christian Middle Class, to apply for your well-being, wealth, and most of all, freedom.

BECOMING SHREWD

Remember the story about the frog and boiling water? Do not try to put a frog in a pot of boiling water. That frog is no dummy; it will jump out.

Rather, start with cool water and slowly turn up the heat. The gradual increase of heat will be accepted by Mr. Frog, and he will allow himself to be boiled to death.

That is what has happened to men and women of faith. We live in a culture that is hostile to us (while appearing to be friendly) and have received countless messages as to what is "normal." Very subtly we have been instructed how we can have it all, our faith and our cultural icons—the current fashions, the latest minivan, the right kind of digital camera.

Am I suggesting that we are victims of a vast financial conspiracy that is attempting to reduce us to financial dust? I am not suggesting it. I am stating it. Is that too strong? Wait and see. The deck is stacked against the Christian Middle Class. If you do not know the money war/game, your strategies will be ineffective and futile. If you know the money war/game, the truth can lead to effective strategies for wealth.

Shrewdness is learned and earned. It is intrinsically spiritual and dynamically practical. It is the ability to rack up impressive spiritual and financial gains in a relatively short period of time. Shrewdness is a life of love, concern, and freedom tempered by attacking the things that threaten our total health. If you are shrewd, you will end up with more money at the end of your month instead of more month at the end of your money. Being shrewd doesn't mean being dishonest, devious, or unscrupulous. On the other hand, it doesn't mean being naive, fearful, or stupid either. It means being able to adapt to circumstances and turn the realities of your life into assets, not liabilities.

Money will not let us go. But we must let it go. We must battle with it until we win. It will be a fight. So let's play to win. We must engage with money on a level playing field, whip it into shape so it will not bother us again, and enjoy the surplus life that comes from having won that battle.

Does the Lord want you to be wealthy? I don't know. Does the Lord want you to be poor? I don't know. I also don't know the circumstances of your life: Do you have cancer? Is your child in a hospital trying to break a drug addiction? Were you a casualty of downsizing at work? I *do* know that the Lord wants you to be truly rich. I can also say that if accident, illness, or disaster does not visit you or your family and you follow the principles in this book, I will scratch my head in wonder if you do not become wealthy.

No, we are not promoting the Prosperity Gospel, and no, I have not lost my mind. Margie and I are truly rich and financially wealthy; not "rich," just wealthy. We had to endure the same things that normal middle-class Christians endure. Our mistakes are your mistakes. Therefore, the logic is simple: Our successes can be your successes.

The other oar is already in hand to put us on a straight course. The oar is shrewdness. Let's get it in the water.

Steps Toward Shrewd

- *Shrewd* means being far-sighted, astute, pragmatic, and wary. When you are shrewd, you are rowing with both oars in the water.
- You need to know where you are now if you're going to make it to shrewd: Are you Financially Alert, Financially Aware, Financially Conscious, or Financially Comatose?
- Jesus tells us to be sheep among wolves, to be *shrewd* as snakes and innocent as doves. The Christian Middle Class is in danger of fulfilling only one part of that equation!
- We will serve money or we will serve Jesus. Therefore, money is the chief competition of Jesus.
- Shrewd Christians do not *ignore* money; nor do they *stop* at money. They go *through* money and get *past* money so they can be involved in more important things.
- You can do this!

The Parable of the Dishonest CFO

He had made it! Rags to riches. From selling used cars to having a personal driver. From being nobody to somebody. From Billy Bob Graves to William ("Call me Will") R. Graves. He had become the Chief Financial Officer of General Radon Dynamic ("GRD" on the NYSE). He had worked hard to get there, no doubt about that, and it had paid off. Nothing was beyond his grasp.

And yet, now that Will had realized his dream, he felt as if things were not quite right. He wanted more, but what? He had taken a chance on coming to the big city. He had been lucky to get a job at GRD. He started, literally, at the lowest entry-level position. Yet he looked back at all of the small jobs as the key to his success. Whatever the position, no matter how seemingly insignificant, he did much more than what was required of him. If anything, he was more than faithful in the little details. He continued that practice, took advantage of the company's generous educational assistance, and discovered that he had a talent for numbers.

His career exploded and he came under the tutelage of a few of the players near the top. A chance elevator conversation with the owner/chairman of the company, James Carter, resulted in further conversations and a new position on the executive floor. Will applied the same principle to his new duties; he did more than was asked of him. Even so, things were not as complete as he thought they should be.

It finally dawned on him. He had made his boss, James Carter, rich. It was true that his boss had been very generous. But the boss was now enjoying life without the sacrifice that Will continued to make. That was not fair.

Will had an idea. The more he thought about it, the more he liked it: adrenaline, strategy, preparation, and risk. James would be tamed. And transferring wealth from the corporation to his offshore accounts would quiet the internal unease. It seemed too good to be true.

Will did an intricate audit of possible corporate vulnerabilities. Ah, the worldwide agricultural division, run by the dimmest of wits: Bob, James's son-in-law. Will began a friendship with Bob that quickly became a mentoring relationship. He taught Bob a lot about the business world. After that, a little flattery and a few ideas really paid off for Bob's division, and Bob was in Will's corner if not in his pocket. The time came to suggest that the bottom line could be enhanced if they removed the current accounting firm. Will had his eye on an up-and-coming group that would do a better job for less money. Bob's corporate reputation had increased as a result of his mentor. Bob thought, *If a new accounting firm will help further my reputation, let's get it done.* After all, Will was being very good to him. What did he or the company have to worry about?

Phase I was firmly in place. Initially uneasy, Bob and his family had come to regard Will as a big brother—everyone except for the oldest son, Blake. He was friendly but reserved. Will knew he had not entirely swallowed his bait. *Aw, he's just a kid—nineteen years old. What does he know?*

Time for Phase II. The old accounting firm was removed and the new firm installed for half the money. They would report only to Will; after all, he was the CFO and could relieve Bob of that burden.

It didn't take long for an "irregularity" to show up on the ledgers. Will covered his trail with a few transfers and made a few adjustments to the program. Closer than he would have liked, but he was up to the challenge. The system had been tested and revised and was now foolproof. Show time!

For the next four years the money flowed. No one noticed because

GRD coffers were filling as well. Will was able to talk about his "investments" in vague enough terms that people only grew in their respect for him. He was now a major player in the community. He was nowhere near the philanthropist James was, but he was close. Representatives of non-profits waited for hours to grasp at a straw from the great man.

He had also become more involved at church. At first, it was just part of his cover. Soon he actually began to enjoy St. Peter's. True, the people were a little naive and simple. But they were tolerable. He got on well with the congregation and knew how to work the system. He moved up the spiritual ladder and eventually took the reins from James, who was chairman of trustees at St. Peter's. Things were going well.

Meanwhile, Blake had finished a double major at MIT: computers and accounting. He had traveled the world for a year. Now he was adjusting to life in the States before he began his own accounting firm. When his family and Will's family decided to take an extended trip abroad, he begged out since he had just returned from such a junket. He wanted to relax, read, and think about the future. No one thought that unusual.

Blake wanted to relax, but his idea of relaxation was computers—in this case, the company computers. His reading was data research and investigation rather than novels. His thinking was based on a number of small observations that had disturbed him over the years. He wanted to put his fears to rest, to reassure himself that things really were as they appeared. Two weeks later he had slipped beneath the encrusted layers of financial deception. His observations had been correct. Blake found an astounding discrepancy of one billion dollars in GRD's books! It looked like a very tough spider's web, and the spider resembled their CFO. Blake was angry.

Then he laid the trap. He scheduled a gigantic return dinner celebration. It was a catered event, no expense spared. The landscape was immaculate: perfect double-mowed grass, new plantings of flowers in full bloom, the immaculately groomed house staff waited outside for the caravan to arrive. The driveway was littered with greens and scented blossoms. Upon arrival, the travelers were set upon by a small army of servers. They brought appetizers: Kumamoto oysters with beluga caviar, crab cakes with chili-lime aioli, plus shrimp, cucumber, and dill-butter canapés. The festivities eased into the house where a classical string quartet provided entertainment. A movie theater was set up in the living room so that as people mingled they could see edited videos of the trip. James was a little puzzled at Blake's extravagance; it wasn't like him. But he was his grandson, and they would chat later.

Dinner was finally served. Gazpacho with lobster and mussels was followed by truffle-studded balsamic foie gras with bitter greens. The entrée—roast goose and appropriate accompaniments—was a surprise to all except Blake. Everyone noticed the unusual entrée, but the evening was going so well, no one said a word. Dessert, however, set their puzzled stomachs at ease: a semifrozen panne cotta served over a warm chocolate mousse with cranberry sauce.

The festivities went on for three hours. Then Blake sprang the trap. The lights dimmed. A spotlight shone on the movie screen that all could see. In the spotlight was a head shot of Will. Everyone smiled at Blake. An acknowledgment of this loyal employee in front of the whole family was fitting.

Blake began, "To our big brother, William R. Graves. He has taken the whole family under his wing, and we are the richer for it. We do appreciate his expertise."

"Here, here!" came the cry.

"While you were gone, I had a great adventure. I was able to read, relax, and think, just as I said I would. My subject of research and discovery was the corporate books of GRD."

Silence. Will's eyes grew wide.

"It turns out that Will has made us all richer; that is the absolute truth. And he was famously compensated for that work. It also turns out that only the first part of my opening statement is true: 'He has taken us!'

To the tune of one billion dollars, some of which I managed to trace to an offshore account. His accounting firm is a bunch of hired guns who ran his program."

The screen dropped the CFO's image. Numbers appeared. And for the next twenty minutes Blake showed a portion of his evidence. Then the screen went blank. The dining room lights came on. Bedlam. Everyone was shaken to the core.

James took over. He turned to Bob and said he hoped the figures were wrong and demanded a full accounting of every detail within the next thirty days. He looked at Will and said: "I should fire you on the spot, but you have been loyal and did make this a great company. Let's hope the new audit is kinder to you than what we have seen here tonight."

Will had been trumped. Anger surged through him as he ran to his Bentley. The little snit. How could he do this to me? Then it hit him. He had stolen a billion dollars. He might go to jail. Who would trust him? Everything was gone. Anger turned to fear and fear turned to panic. He was too old to start over. No one would ever partner with him. Then a new plan began to form. Risky? Certainly! But the alternative was a lot worse.

For the next month he went after receivables with a vengeance. He told his Saudi clients, "You owe 500 million barrels of oil. If you settle accounts today, you will only need to deliver 350 million." He called Brazil. "You owe 300,000 head of cattle. If you close today, you only need to deliver 225,000." He made similar calls to South Africa, France, Russia, Taiwan, Israel, Colombia, and Australia. Everyone agreed to his deals. He figured that if he worked out such deals, he would be welcome in those international communities after he left GRD.

At the end of the thirty days, he walked into the conference room. He was not invited to speak. Instead, the floor was given to a new accounting firm, and Blake was the presenter. Everything was there in black and white, including the details about Will's latest shenanigans with the receivables. His heart sank. He was going to jail.

James took the podium. When he began to talk, he sounded firm and disappointed but not outraged. The audience noticed his demeanor. "Will, we gave you great compensation, the run of the company, and our friendship. You have betrayed our trust. You are fired. In no way will I commend your dishonesty. I must admit that I have always liked the way you could develop and execute your plans. If you had stayed straight, we could have rebuilt the world. But you turned crooked. There are two verses in the Old Testament that are the same word for word; one in 2 Samuel and one in Psalms. They state that the Lord will deal shrewdly with the crooked. I am turning you over to Him. I will let Him take vengeance."

Then James took on a more thoughtful tone and surprised everyone with his next words: "On the other hand, I must commend you for your shrewdness in dealing with your present situation. You used money to build relationships that would ensure your survival. After all, the purpose of money is for relationships. It has no inherent use on its own. I wish I could get that through to the folks at St. Peter's. They are not close to being as wise in handling money as you are. I sometimes wonder who will trust them with true riches if they cannot handle a temporary thing like money.

"I know what I'm saying must be a surprise to people here. But shrewdness is how I started this business. I wasn't dishonest, but I had to be shrewd to get the most leverage possible. I had to be as wise as a snake and as innocent as a dove. Not an easy agenda. Yet I did it. Will, your betrayal has really helped my understanding. Early on in my career, I thought being rich was success, that money was what mattered. That money was how you kept score.

"Later I began to realize that success could be defined best if money was not in the picture. Now, thanks to you, my thinking has been kicked up a notch: I see now that money is the chief competition of Jesus; you will serve one or the other. I didn't want to believe it. I fought it. But this whole turn of events is the final nail in the coffin."

Then in a firm, loud voice he punctuated each word: "The truth is, you cannot serve both God and money. You will hate the one and love the other. Period. There is no other way!"

Then James spoke to Will: "You are gone from this corporation. You have been dishonest, and you must go. However, I appreciate your shrewd audacity. There will be no jail time."

Blake stood aloof, looking amused at his grandfather. The rest of the family didn't understand what they saw. Everyone wanted blood. They began an angry clamor. James simply stared back at them. One by one they became quiet. It didn't seem fair. But James was the boss. It was over.

A STRANGE PARABLE

The above parable may sound familiar to you. It is based on a parable Jesus told in Luke 16:1-14. How did Will Graves, though dollar rich, lose by not being truly rich? How can we as the CMC learn from that story? How can we learn to be truly rich and financially wealthy?

Will had learned from experience that what he possessed never equaled "enough." He thought that life meant something "out there," an external that would take his internal frustration away. His purchased toys, whether cars, planes, islands, or corporations, never were "enough." Surely the big takeaway from GRD would give him the internal psychic income for which he lusted. He played the game he learned from his culture.

Years ago a great preacher, Helmut Thielecke, wrote that the secret to understanding the New Testament was to put yourself in the place of every person who encountered the Lord. He felt that each person Jesus encountered represented a part of us. When we could identify that core within us, the scripture would come alive. As hard as it is for us to believe, William R. Graves is a part of you and me. In smaller ways we can identify with him just as we can identify with the man in Jesus' parable.

Our temptation is to believe the culture and think of life as something external—we are our possessions—as opposed to something internal—we are our relationships, beliefs, and values. As Jesus said, "The kingdom of God is within you" (Luke 17:21).

Will's actions are our potential; they lurk as the underbelly to our souls. After all, haven't we all felt that at times our situation is "unfair"? Haven't we all been tempted to do something about it? Perhaps some of us *have* done something about it. Perhaps we are not proud of what we've done.

The words of James Carter are, per my paraphrase, the words of Jesus. (You might be able to put them in another form. Have at it. Working on that story is a life-changing event.) This parable has bothered Christians for a long time. It may seem that Jesus was commending the dishonesty of the administrator, but in reality, Jesus was commending his shrewdness.

We cannot serve God and money. The only way to serve God is to go through money, conquer it, put it in its proper place, and catch up to the Lord's plan for our lives. In this parable Jesus was illustrating the reality of money and its impact on our lives. It cannot and should not be worshiped, nor should it be ignored.

You might be thinking, *Hold it, Neil. You have gone too far. My circumstances do not allow me to ignore money; far from it. I can't worship money; I don't make or have enough to worship it. Worshiping money is the job of the rich. I can't do it on my salary. As a good Christian, I do* not *serve money.*

I would agree that you do not make a habit of bowing at the altar of money. You do not worship money consciously. However, you might continually desire the "better" things of life. Perhaps you have credit-card debt. Perhaps you give very little to the Lord's work. Perhaps you have zero reserves for emergencies or retirement. Perhaps the catalogs for your favorite hobby get more attention than the Bible does.

If you live in the land of contentment and generosity rather than the land of getting, not focusing on things you "need," then you are correct: You have mastered money. (Why don't you see if the store that sold you this book will give you your money back?)

Okay, time for the financial confessions of a repentant financial sinner: I am a recovering moneyholic. Having personally experienced most of the financial sins (laziness, ignorance, greed, fear, etc.), I am fully aware of the subtle, insidious poison of money. Money cannot give us the intrinsic, internal completeness that we all desire. It cannot lead us to life. Green paper is not a power. It has no real worth; it has symbolic worth. Money is what we make of it, and there are only two choices: (1) we are either the servants of God and the masters of money to advance that service, or (2) we are not.

STEPS TOWARD SHREWD

- Jesus did not commend dishonesty, but He did commend shrewdness.
- More is never enough.
- The purpose of money is to build relationships and serve us. If we think that the purpose of money is to have money or, even more damning, to appear to have money, we are serving money. As Jean-Paul Sartre said, "We are possessed by the things we possess."
- Little things mean a lot. If we are faithful in little things, big things will be entrusted to us. If we are not faithful in little things, big things will not be entrusted to us.
- If we cannot handle worldly wealth, we will not become truly rich.
- To get to true riches, we must go through, not around or without, money.
- Money is an impostor that promises life but never delivers.
- We must have a plan to attain true riches; we must become Shrewd Christians.

Toughing It Out

The first step toward shrewdness is to recognize that we are in a financial war—a war that most in the middle class are losing. The second step is to recognize that counterfeits of shrewdness will try to confuse and derail us. Some are from our worldly culture, and some are from our Christian culture. Each attempts to steal our joy, our inheritance, and our life. Each is deadly.

FIVE COUNTERFEITS THAT WILL RIP YOUR HEART OUT

Greed

Greed is the major cultural counterfeit of shrewd. In the movie *Wall Street,* the antagonist, Gordon Gekko, makes the statement: "Greed is good." He might have been the prototype of an Enron executive—or our next-door neighbor. At times, he might be a prototype for you and me.

Contrast that with Jesus' statement: "Be on your guard against all kinds of greed; a man's life does not consist in the abundance of his possessions" (Luke 12:15).

Greed is *not* good. It is *never* good. Humans should learn this over time. We never seem to grasp the fact that greed, in any form, is a bad deal. It always gets us into trouble. Greed is about taking unscrupulous advantage of another person. Greed or lust (take your pick) for many CMCers can be spelled f-a-s-h-i-o-n or a-u-t-o-m-o-b-i-l-e.

Shrewdness is not greed.

Fear

A great verse in the Bible puts it very succinctly: "Perfect love drives out fear" (1 John 4:18). Let's put that verse in reverse: "Perfect fear drives out love." It works, doesn't it? From that, we can conclude that the opposite of fear is love. Fear drives a wedge into our relationships. It comes through finances in particular.

Many people fear life is passing them by; they do not have "enough." Therefore, they need more money to fund the lifestyle they think they deserve. The things that money has bought enslave them. They are consumed with consumption.

Others fear the future will be disastrous. They feel they must hoard their money or get the absolute maximum dollar out of every investment. In this case, money itself has ensnared them; their lifestyle is cheap and miserly.

When we fall for either of these fears (or dozens of others), money creates a hold on us—usually at the expense of our families. I remember being resentful of the mixed money messages my parents gave me. One day money was growing on trees and I could have as much as I wanted; the next day, my parents were yelling at me for spending money. I was a child, and I didn't know anything about the closely guarded family income secret. I didn't know that at times we were flush and at other times nearly broke. Instead, I was confused about money and began to adopt the fears of my parents.

Financial fears spread their virus, infecting us, our families, and all who come into contact with us. If we live paycheck to paycheck for years on end, we have an aching dread that life could come crashing down on us. When a recession hits, that dull ache turns into a persistent stress that affects how we relate to our families.

Financial Alertness is different than fear. When you're alert, you are letting money serve you. When you are in fear, you are in bondage to something that shouldn't have that much control.

Bad Shepherds

The Bible talks about believers as sheep. John Paul Getty said, "Because God made sheep, He expects them to be sheared." It sounds as if Getty was talking to the CMC. Sheep essentially need leadership. Jesus is the Good Shepherd. If we follow Him, we will be visiting adventurous, beautiful, and fulfilling destinations. Figuratively speaking, we will see great valleys with plenty to eat and drink and unbelievable relaxation. When the inevitable tension and difficulty arrive, we will not be left to our own devices.

It stands to reason that if there is a Good Shepherd we will also encounter Bad Shepherds along the way. The Bad Shepherds lead us to the wolves, not the place of beauty, rest, enjoyment, and plenty. And then, when we are safely in the hands of the wolves, they desert us to find another flock to lead astray. (Let the reader note that my distaste for Bad Shepherds is so great that I will use the initials "BSers" to describe them. "BS," as you know, is slang for "Baloney Sausage.")

There are four kinds of Bad Shepherds in our world. They coordinate with one another, and their purpose is to destroy you. Now don't get me wrong. They are just doing their jobs. Some even have good intentions. But remember that you need to be alert to their messages or you will not be heading toward true riches.

1. *Advertisers* connect the dots from the products they are hawking to our most basic human needs. They want us to buy, buy, buy. For example, the auto industry often uses advertisements showing sexy women in sleek cars because they want your money. Last time I checked, I did not see any of these women in the passenger seats of new cars.

2. *Marketers* discover pleasing arrangements that lure us into stores to buy, buy, buy. There is even a professional known as a Merchandising Display Expert who is responsible for arranging displays in windows and throughout stores in such a way as to attract customers.

3. *Retailers* train salespeople to sell. I call this the "meat strategy." The salespeople are the wolves, and we are the sheep (a.k.a. "the meat"). What is more intimidating than wearing jeans to purchase a new suit from an impeccably attired wolf in a fancy department store? They want you to buy, buy, buy.

4. *Merchants of Misery* are the financiers who push debt at you every way they can.[1] (They have the nerve to call them "credit" cards.) "No money? No problem! We take Visa, MasterCard, Discover, American Express—or we will give you 10 percent off if you open an account with us today. We can open an account in just five minutes." They want you to buy, buy, buy.

The BSer's job is to lead you, gently, slowly, surely into a life of insatiable and insidious desire. They create these desires by matching products to your deepest needs through commercials and ads that promise life but do not deliver. But they promise so much on the way that you want to walk with them. Our constant exposure to "stuff" through these avenues leads to an unconscious belief that we must have more.

I call this brainwashing. According to my dictionary, *brainwashing* is "a forcible indoctrination to induce someone to give up basic religious beliefs and attitudes to accept contrasting regimented ideas," or secondarily, "persuasion by propaganda or salesmanship." Brainwashing does not merely point you to products, it gets you to visit the wolves.

The wolves are out to devour you. Their slogan is, "Image is everything; you can have it all!" Because so many Christians are naturally trusting, they are fair game for greedy people in the marketplace. Especially if the salespeople are well trained and the sheep have no immune system to protect them from that training.

Let me give you an example: housing. Everyone needs shelter. One Saturday with nothing better to do, you look at the housing section of the newspaper. It shows smiling people in beautiful, "affordable" housing. And a great mortgage rate. Why throw money away on rent? You can't build equity and wealth by renting. (Of course you can, but no one wants you to know that.)

It won't hurt to just "look." You aren't doing anything anyway. You saunter into an open house, and the wolf—er, agent—smiles, goes through a few preliminaries, and gets down to business. "What price range were you looking at? What is your income? Why, you can afford *this!*"

You reply, "Wow! We can? What an unbelievable rate! It's too good to be true!"

This is when the wolf introduces you to MOM: the Merchant of Misery, your friendly mortgage broker. When it comes time for closing, you find that there are a few financial odds and ends that need to be tidied up—$10 there, $50 here, $330 over here, $5 there. But the lender smiles and says, "Why don't we wrap them all into the mortgage? That way you won't be paying anything out of pocket, and your mortgage payments will be tax deductible for many years to come!" What a great deal…for MOM. The Bad Shepherd caught your attention with an ad. You pranced out to the wolves. The wolves ate you and brought what was left to MOM. And you thought you got a deal.

Almost assuredly you paid too much. Your real-estate agent collected not from you but from the seller. *What's that? She works for the seller? She may not have had my best interests at heart?* She is a wolf. The banker wrapped fees into your mortgage generating more profit for him and less for you. But the excitement of having a home is simply too much. Honest, she didn't look like a wolf…

When our nature collides with the BSers of our culture, we tend to lose money. When we are *sad,* we pick up a self-help or inspirational book and a Caramel Macchiato from Starbucks. When we are *glad,* we buy presents for those we love. When we are *mad,* we buy something for ourselves. When we are *bad,* we bring home guilt offerings. When we have been *had,* we buy an embarrassment eraser. When we ignore the *pad,* we look for a new home… And on it goes. (If we do buy another pad, we can be *sad, bad, glad, mad, and had* all in one transaction!)

I made the mistake of skipping a grade in elementary school. It made sense academically, but the purpose of school appears to be socialization, not education. I became the youngest kid in my grade. I went from being able to hold my own physically to not quite being fit for the top rungs of athletics. Consequently, other kids constantly bullied me. I didn't like that part of growing up at all.

Today I like it even less. But the bullies of today are corporations. They are attempting to take whatever they can from you—and then some. They conspire to fleece you. They know they win if they make a profit, and you and your money are their means to that end.

It's nothing personal; they are not after *you* per se, just your money. If they happen to put you in the bondage of excruciating debt and they end up with you as well as your money, well, so be it. And if in the process, your relationships with your wife, family, and friends decline, well, shoot, you still have that quality sound system to soothe the pain of a broken family.

Comparison and Competition

Remember the Joneses? The family you've been trying to keep up with? Well, the Joneses retired from their leadership position years ago. They became too exhausted to continue playing the game. They are now living under the Witness Protection Program as a consequence of all the trouble they caused.

So it is no longer the Joneses' living standard that dictates the money game; the game has expanded outside our neighborhood to affinity groups. An affinity group is a group with whom we want to identify. We find affinity groups in the workplace, in the play place, at church, on television, on the radio, and so on. Their messages come at such a confusing, furious pace that our sensibilities are knocked aside. The affinity group determines the rules of our lifestyle.

In each new season of life, we upgrade our standard of consumption. Brett Posten and Robert TenEyck of Ideocore, a Southern California advertising agency, illustrate this phenomenon with the following advertising creations of affinity groups:

> When I was 13, I accepted MTV into my heart.
>
> When I was 23, I accepted Nike into my heart.
>
> When I was 33, I accepted BMW into my heart.
>
> When I was 43, I accepted Forbes into my heart.
>
> When I was 53, I accepted Vail into my heart.
>
> When I was 63, I accepted Viagra into my heart.[2]

Affinity groups let us know that we "belong" by the way we dress, talk, drive, eat, and drink. (You are aware, aren't you, that Coca-Cola spends big money if Brad Pitt or Harrison Ford actually takes a drink of Coke in his latest movie? After all, Coca-Cola has to stay ahead of Pepsi.)

Affluenza is the financial virus that has entrapped the CMC into enslavement to money. This virus communicates the Cultural Gospel that you are nothing if you do not have a lot of things. But since the things you have are never enough, you always need more things. And *better*— don't forget better. You are in a world that surrounds you with lifestyle choices that link you inextricably to the service of money. The answer is always more money! Why? It just is, that's all!

These soft, subtle messages create space in our minds for which they pay no rent. They tell us: *There is more to life. You are special. You are deserving of the VERY best.* Constant bombardment will brainwash anyone to the point where he or she can be manipulated.

What purchases have you made recently because blatant, continuous, and pervasive messages suggested that an upgrade was in your best interest? For instance, let's say you know that you cannot afford a BMW. Your budget says you can afford a four-year-old used Chevrolet. You find what you can afford on the lot. But wait. What a deal the salesperson has for you! Did you know there's 0 percent financing on *new* Chevrolets? *Golly, it must be the Lord guiding us to this opportunity. More car! Cool! Payments are the same, though the coupon book may be around a little longer. But hey, I am a King's Kid; I deserve it.* You might be proud that you didn't succumb to the BMW temptation, but you still bought more than you could afford.

Why do inner-city kids wear $200 shoes and $100 gold necklaces? Why does the CMC buy too much house or car or spend too much for a private school? Why do the rich take advantage of them?

Were you aware that the number one cultural activity in our country is shopping? A visit to the mall is standard operating procedure for more and more people. Yet, when surveyed, 75 percent of the people at the mall had not come with a planned purchase! This means that there is a strong connection between yesterday's brainwashing and today's impulse buying!

The diagram below is circular and constantly swirling in our lives. Our culture is built on comparison and competition, which lead to deprived feelings, which lead to a demand for action, which in turn leads to the purchase of consumer goods. The satisfaction of consumer goods only works for one day, and then we are back in the cycle again. Sound fun?

Comparison plus competition leads to consumption. The truth is that

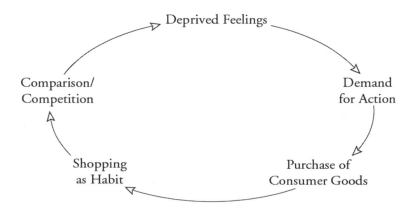

you are comparing yourself to what the BSers have *said* you should have. What would happen if you compare yourself to the global economy? Every year America's teenagers are *given* more money by their parents than the lowest quartile of the world *earns* in that same year. You wouldn't know that by listening to the BSers! According to them you *need* more, you *deserve* more, and you will only be fulfilled if you *get* more.

Unbiblical Counterfeits Posing as Legitimate Scriptural Guides
Shrewd Christians do not believe in the following errors:

1. *The Poverty Gospel*—"Okay, I am a total failure at handling my finances. I will make a virtue out of it, spiritualize it, and pretend that wealth has nothing to do with money. I will prove that I am spiritually better than you by pointing out my simplicity and humility." It was Socrates who once mocked such a person, saying, "I can see your vanity through the holes in your cloak."

2. *The Presumptive Gospel*—"Okay, God wants us to live like His children. He does not want us to go without. He wants us to have the best. Therefore, because we associate with people at work, and they do these fun vacations and drive this kind of car, we should not deny ourselves this treat. Unless, of course, the Lord doesn't want us to have it. So we prayed about it, and Jesus did not show up in person to tell us no. Therefore, He wants us to have it, and He will provide the means to pay for it." (*Please note:* The Presumptive Gospel can also take the form of: "I don't believe in life insurance; I am just going to trust the Lord." Sing it with me, "Na-Na Nah, Nah, Na-Na Nah, Nah, HEY, HEY, HEY, Good-bye.")

3. *The Prosperity Gospel*—"Okay, God, I did what You asked. I gave You some of my hard-earned cash; now You are *obligated* to bless me. Where is it?"

How many people have you known who have become victims of crooks who came to them as "experts" in the name of Jesus? We continue to fall for the investment scams that promise "a high rate of interest with *no* risk!" because a slick-talking "born-againer" mugs us with the pitch and prayer. We must stop listening to the scam artists. We must become our own financial consultants and never again invest in anything we don't understand.

THE GANG OF THREE

So far I have been blasting a part of the economic system that would enslave us and make money our master. I am not against capitalism. It is a flawed system, but it is certainly better than any other option. The truth is, any financial option would work if it were not for the reality of sin. My hope is that you will become aware of the inherent, subtle dangers that amount to financial brainwashing. If, as a member of the CMC, buying things has become an additional source of your identity, you have learned to leave your faith at home as you head to the mall. When you do that, the Gang of Three is waiting to further derail your life.

Gang Member One. It will not shock you to understand that our *self-centeredness* gets in the way of our fully enjoying the life that Jesus promised. The Bible term is *flesh.* When we live in flesh, we can be small, independent, selfish little nasties! When push comes to shove, it is everyone for self; faith and relationship be damned. Literally. I heard a speaker define *flesh* as "learned independence from God." In other words, when we live in the flesh after we've committed our lives to Christ, we are employing the same strategies we used for survival *before* we trusted Christ.

Gang Member Two. It may have shocked you to see the ruthless and predatory strategy the *culture* employs for the sake of profit. The Bible term is *world.* When we are *of* the culture, we get caught up in patterns that gently, slowly, and seductively lead us to confusion and then to disaster. The culture is constantly repatterning our minds to fit in the way the culture says we should. The war is stacked against us. Big time!

Gang Member Three. It will not shock you to understand that we have an *Enemy,* our Adversary who wants to undo our faith. The Bible term is *the devil.* He is not nice. And he is good at what he does, which is to confuse, to lie, to tempt, and to accuse. His goal for us is to "steal and kill and destroy" (John 10:10). That doesn't sound nice, does it?

The Gang of Three, whether they enter our lives by invitation or force, will do what they do best: wreak havoc. Picture a vise in your mind. You know, that tool on your dad's workbench that held things tightly. Perhaps you wondered what would happen if you tightened the vise on your little finger. (If you did tighten it on your finger, you didn't wonder long. It hurt!)

For this illustration, think of one side of the vise as *The Culture* and the other side as *The Enemy.* I know you are not clueless. You have already figured out that *Self-centeredness* sits in the middle. Once that handle starts turning, we start twisting and dancing as both sides move together to crush the life out of us. The pain is indescribable.

We allow outside forces to combine with our internal nature to trap us *in* money and, consequently, to stop us *at* money and move us toward *confusion.* Our lives, our families, and our faith are impaired. We are becoming an endangered species. And we have to get out of this mess on our own.

How do we do that? Truth and assistance. Truth means that we must invest in new information to counter our Adversary, the culture, and our selfishness. Truth always has and always will make us free. Assistance means that we must link up with the Power that is much greater than that of our Enemy. No contest there. If we do discover new truth and God's explosiveness, we will discover what it means to be fully alive. We can ask Him questions, even silly questions, and He will respond without making us feel foolish or guilty.

Our goal is to have life. God's goal is to give it to us. His idea of life is far better than our idea of life (which was largely shaped by our friendly culture and the Enemy.) We are wise when we move toward His idea of life.

TABLE MANNERS

In polite society it is important to have a basic understanding of appropriate dining etiquette. It will probably not impress a potential employer that you can eat your peas with your knife. Likewise, your future in-laws may not watch approvingly as you lick that last bit of lobster bisque out of the bowl.

In this book, Table Manners will refer to something beyond common etiquette. They will remind us of what each of us must bring to the table in order to master money and get beyond it.

There are four elements that comprise Table Manners: coachability, enthusiasm, ingenuity, and toughness. Each stands alone, but they all work together. You get the most if you apply all four, consistently and continuously. You do not need to bring brilliance to the table. You do not need an education. You *do* need to be on the same page with your spouse (if you are married) or at least moving in that direction (see chapter 5). And you may want to bring earplugs. Your stockbroker cousin Sidney is going to try to convince you that there is a better way. (Of course, that would be *his* way.)

Learning these Table Manners will get you started in the right direction toward becoming a certified SC (Shrewd Christian). The concept is "more life, less money." Here we go.

1. Coachability. We need to admit that we do not have all the answers. We need to be willing to step out of previous habits that have put us into a rut. (*Rut:* a grave with open ends.) Being coachable means that we are willing to learn new strategies. Do not think budget; budgets only work for disciplined, systematic people. There is a better way for the rest of us. If we are serving money, we need to admit that and decide we want to get things turned around.

2. Enthusiasm. No, Marsha, please put away your U of Missouri cheerleader outfit. That kind of enthusiasm has no staying power. We do not need to play-act.

We *do* need to understand that enthusiasm is the heartbeat of success. It means, literally, God within us. Think of it in those terms. Picture yourself achieving the goal of taming the money monster. You will have to be upbeat about your new life. (Check out Philippians 2:10-12. As you work out this area of your salvation, God will empower you.)

3. Ingenuity. Being ingenious means that we recognize the genius within. Each of us has personal financial genius waiting to happen. It is not brain surgery. Think about it. Genius is nothing more than simplicity expanded. (After all, think how much has developed because of the wheel!) Now it is your turn to make your life work—on *your* terms, not the terms of the culture.

I like to cook. I like recipes, but I usually adapt them to what I have on hand. In other words, recipes are starting places. They are not ending places. The plan for shrewdness is like a cookbook. The recipes are there, but it is up to you, if necessary, to adapt them to your particular reality. What you bring to the table will make or break your complete success.

I wish life were simple, but it isn't. Life is difficult. Simplistic financial formulas do not work for every person. Therefore, like cooking recipes, they need to be adjusted to whatever is necessary for success. If the formulas here don't work for your particular circumstances, adjust and expand them to make them work.

4. Toughness. Surprised? We are not talking gridiron courage here; this is not "smash-mouth finance." We are talking about the courage to hang in and hang on when the going gets rough. Of the four Table Manners, toughness is by far the most important one.

All of us are energized by the thought of mastering money. We all like to make plans for success. We probably have had such thoughts and plans about other things in life. We have usually failed miserably. The diet, the exercise program, the study group… What will make *this* program different is toughness.

Let's spend a little more time on toughness. It will take a lot of toughness to win the war, and I want to be sure you know you are up for it. Let's ponder the following verse for a moment: "They will soar on wings like eagles; they will run and not grow weary, they will walk and not be faint" (Isaiah 40:31).

"Soar on wings like eagles." Who wouldn't like to soar above the mediocre turkeys around us? There is great joy (to say nothing of pride) when a few people achieve the title of "eagle." They are the superb few. They are an admired group of people because of what they accomplish.

"Run and not grow weary." Have you read of the people who get their kicks running ultramarathons—one hundred miles across the desert—and other such torture events? They are in fabulous condition. Their resting pulse is about twelve, and they have a body fat measurement of minus 5 percent. They are an admired group of people because of what they have accomplished.

"Walk and not be faint." How bland; how boring. Who could admire the plodders? *Anybody* can walk. That is true. It is also true that the key is to walk and not give up. The walkers do not have the crowd admiring them and urging them to succeed. The walkers plod alone and have to put one foot in front of the other. They have to believe in themselves and the goal.

Isn't it interesting that the walkers share the same verse as the eagles and the runners and are as honored as the first two groups?

Walkers have to be tough. So do you.

I enjoy speaking to a variety of audiences. One year I spoke at a camp that majored in adventure. Every person in the camp had to go through a high-ropes course. Needless to say, there were a lot of white knuckles in the camp; many campers wept or swore or both. But everyone did the course. A great accomplishment.

During my talk the night of that experience, I asked three questions. After mentioning the high ropes course, I asked, "How many of you were not scared even one little bit?" Boom, up went a lot of macho hands, the toughest of the tough…or so they thought.

Then I asked, "How many of you were really scared and did it anyway?" The rest of the campers cautiously, timidly, and slowly raised their hands.

I then posed my final question, "Which group showed more toughness: the ones who were not scared and did the ropes, or the ones who were scared and did the ropes anyway?" The light began to dawn.

If you do something and are not scared, what you accomplish doesn't have anything to do with toughness. But if you do something and are scared before, during, and after, what you accomplish takes great toughness—staying the course when everything is screaming at you to pack it in. Tough; that is you. Shrewd is coming up!

MAKING THE CHOICE

You can choose to bring these qualities to the table. Or not. You can choose to be shrewd. Or not. You can select a lifestyle that will work for you. Or not.

Everyone follows a financial plan and spends income in a certain way. If you do not have a conscious plan in place, *you have chosen to let others make the plan for you* . Last time I checked human nature, that may not be the best option. (Unbelievable, but true: Many people do not have a will. If you are one of those people, this means you are choosing to let the state handle your assets when you die.)

The choice most middle-income people make is to let other people call the shots. This results in financial claustrophobia. Shrewd people have a good financial plan. This moves them from claustrophobia to confidence.

Think about this: You're wandering in the forest and get lost. You find that you have somehow gotten wrapped up in a sticky, gooey mess. It's dark. You can't move. You rest a moment and realize you're not dead. The struggle begins. You find a weak point in the mess. You struggle some more and eventually you see light. More struggles and you are free.

Now that you have escaped the mess, you are determined not to ever be caught like that again. You begin to walk away victoriously. But something feels strange. The struggle has caused you to develop new musculature. Instead of looking down, for the first time in your life you look up! At that very moment the wind catches you and you fly. You have just been transformed from a caterpillar into a soaring butterfly. You are, literally, a whole new being because you toughed out the struggle.

Your life, especially the financial aspect, may resemble an insect barely able to crawl. You may find yourself in a dark, gooey, confining financial cocoon. And you may have given up. Unlike the caterpillar, you may not automatically struggle with all your might to break free. You may have given a feeble attempt, but now are resigned to this cocoon that has created the permanent condition of financial claustrophobia. You can stay there facing the dark mess and all of its limitations. Or you can enter into a struggle and break free into a new life.

Most of us think that being tough means gritting our teeth, becoming very uncomfortable, and going through agony. In other words, doing something tough is not a pleasant experience. Au contraire: Our modus operandi is "more life, less money." But only the tough will finish this race and win.

Steps Toward Shrewd

- The counterfeits of shrewdness will keep you from becoming wealthy: greed, fear, Bad Shepherds, comparison and competition, and unbiblical counterfeits posing as financial guides.
- Our constant exposure to "stuff" brainwashes us, confuses us, and leads to an unconscious belief that we must have more.

- Comparison plus competition leads to consumption.
- Become your own financial consultant.
- Selfishness, the culture, and the Enemy conspire to keep us from becoming wealthy.
- We need to be coachable, enthusiastic, ingenious, and tough to become wealthy.
- Toughness is the most important quality.
- You have to *choose* to become shrewd.

The Road to Contentment

I recently taught a course on money at a seminary. There was a very handsome couple in the class. I asked the husband, "Peter, if you could drive any car you wanted and didn't have to pay for it, what would it be?"

Without hesitation and with a wide grin, he replied, "A Ford F-250 V-8 pickup truck, every option, extended cab, four-wheel drive with a topper and a ski rack."

I smiled back and said, "Should we make it diesel?"

Bigger grin. "Yeah, let's make it diesel."

"Okay, I want to be sure I have this straight. Your dream vehicle is a free brand-new Ford F-250 pickup truck, diesel-powered, four-wheel drive, all available options, extended cab, topper, and ski rack. Did I miss anything?"

"No, that ought to do it. When do I get it?"

The class laughed and so did I…after reminding him that this was an illustration.

My next question was a fireball.

"Peter, you may have a new Ford just like the one you described *every* year for the rest of your life; however, the trade-off of having this truck is that you will *never* be content. Or you can drive a 1996 Ford Taurus that has seen better days. The trade-off of driving this car is that you will *always* be content. Peter, which do you choose?"

Peter sat there stunned. He hadn't thought about contentment. And when his options were presented in those terms, he didn't know what to choose! His thinking had always been, *When I get to this level and have these things, then I will be content.* Was that his conscious thinking? No. Was it his practical behavior? Yes. As is true for most of us.

We have been conditioned by our culture, even our Christian culture, to believe that our contentment is something "out there." It usually follows a "when" strategy: "When I find the right person…" "When I get the right job…" "When I have kids…" "When we can afford to move to a larger house…" "When we can afford to retire…" Isn't it interesting that all these strategies have to do with money? "When" never gets here.

True contentment means having *life*. Jesus talked about life—not survival, not existence. To further sharpen our understanding, listen to Him speak in John 10:10: "The thief comes to steal, kill and destroy. But I have come to bring you life and far more life than you have experienced before" (Atkinson's Revised Version). Life is found in uproarious proactive advancement that holds boredom at bay. Life is more than just being alive. Irenaeus, one of the early church fathers, said it best: "The glory of God is a person *fully* alive."

It is true that we live on earth and not heaven. Consequently, we will have realities that disappoint us: job difficulties, job politics, difficult neighbors, barking parrots (seriously, they are a neighborhood nuisance!), and so on. But we experience life on the inside, not the outside—the kingdom of God is within you. Consequently, outside things do not determine whether or not our cup is full.

One more illustration. Let's say that you have just purchased a new home, and you have your best friends over for a tour.

"Wow!"

Smile. "Yep!"

"New furniture, new appliances, central vacuuming. Is that what I think it is? One of the state-of-the-art systems that automatically adjusts lighting, heating, and cooling to your personal preset instructions wherever you are in the house? It's initiated by your body temperature and movement...it knows your signature."

"Yep!"

"Say, isn't this the model that has tricky walls? You can expand or contract rooms depending on your particular mood of the day?"

"Yep!"

"Did you get this from your brother-in-law, the one who lives in a home for only eighteen months and then builds a newer model? Doesn't he usually give you a great deal?"

"Yep!"

"Whooee! Good deal! A really nice house." Short silence. "Do you have any root beer?"

(In Christian books, it has to be root beer.) And that is the end of impressing your best friend. Took seven minutes. Everyone else you encounter is going to be less impressed in less time. Was that seven minutes worth the effort it took to move into this house? But of course there is more.

The very next week you will be hurrying to work, concentrating on your upcoming deadlines, and you will *forget* the home in which you are living. One week, and the house is not the only thing on your mind. The dream home, car, or vacation cannot provide any more than a moment of satisfaction. When that moment is over, we are off to the next new thing.

Life is not about things. Our consumer-driven economy is about things. If we believe that life is found in the externals as our culture teaches us, we will believe that what we drive tells people who we are. Confusion wants us to believe that there is a thing-size vacuum within us that is waiting for just the "right" thing to fill it.

Confusion eraser: Nothing outside of great relationships (true riches) can satisfy us at our deepest levels.

To expand on what Pascal said, "There is a 'God-sized vacuum' within each of us that cannot be filled by people or things; it can only be filled by God." It is my experience that most CMC people believe Pascal. Or at least they want to, sort of, in an occasional way.

Let's paraphrase Ecclesiastes 5:10-12: "The person who loves to shop never can shop enough. The person who loves to acquire never can acquire enough." It is the search for the Holy Grail. The "grail" does not exist. The search is all that matters. So in our war we find that *having* something does not fill us. It is the implied promise of fulfillment in *getting* that "thing" that draws us.

One New Year's Eve, Margie and I headed to the Penrose Room at the Broadmoor Hotel for dinner. (For those of you who are not falling off your chair in amazement at our destination, the Broadmoor is an exceptional five-star hotel in Colorado Springs.) We enjoyed our meal. (I am glad we did; it cost more than my first car.) But I was bothered by something as I was leading Margie out to the dance floor for our annual dance. (We dance one time per year to prove we are saved by grace.) I finally figured out what was bothering me. Margie and I were excited to be there. It was a special night. Yet it appeared that we were the only ones in the room enjoying the evening!

Every other couple surrounding the dance floor had placed their party hats on very bored-looking heads. Most were not talking to their tablemates. They had the "been here, done this" look on their faces. As we danced, I whispered something in Margie's ear. She was disappointed in what I said. It was not a sweet nothing; she likes sweet nothings. But it was important. I said, "Hon, look around you. Look at the expressions. This is the charter chapter of OLD—the Organization of the Living Dead. They are gone, but no one has given them permission to lie down. Margie, you're a leader; you tell them it's okay for dead people to lie down."

I was kidding, but Margie did not think I was funny. She gave me "the look," and thus "endeth" the dance. Our fellow revelers had it all, and it wasn't enough. They appeared to be dollar rich and life poor. They did not appear to be truly rich.

We often read articles about people with $100,000 incomes "struggling" to make ends meet. Sad. I know a woman whose former husband sends her *only* $200,000 per year in alimony and child support. How could she possibly live on that trifling amount? Very sad.

I have a client who makes only $32,000 after twenty-five years with the same company. His hobby is his passion. He has more than enough. Glad.

Our daughter, Jodi, worked in an orphanage in Nicaragua. The generator was shut off at nine each night. The orphanage had no hot water, but they made up for it with lots of bats, rats, and mice. There were fifteen kids under the age of two, and total silence prevailed in the compound for only three hours a day. Jodi received room and board for the four months she worked there. No other pay. Very glad.

Life is lived on our insides. What makes our insides smile? More money is almost never the answer. (And no, you are *not* part of the "almost.")

Enough Is What You Have

Most financial authors are very intent on directing you toward learning the difference between your wants and your needs. They feel that this will help you control spending. You know the drill: You *want* something, but do you really *need* it? To be fiscally sound, you must distinguish between your wants and your needs.

Perhaps, but we have heard the need/want thing so often that the words have become a cliché and have no influence on how we purchase things. The wants of yesterday have become the needs of today. Twenty-five years ago, air conditioning in a car was a luxury; today we expect it. Personal computers were not even thought of by most people in the '80s, and now it is assumed that everybody has one. E-mail was a strange concept in the early '90s; today, most of us are online.

Let's approach this from a different angle. Instead of trying to differentiate between needs and wants and the ever-shrinking line that separates them, let's come in the back door.

Ask yourself, What do I lack? Don't ask, What do I need or want that is out there? but rather, What is unavailable to me at the moment that is causing my life distress? What do I lack?

Do you lack faith, shelter, food, transportation, clothing, or relationships? Do you have furniture, hot water, a television? We rarely enter personal crises voluntarily. But they help us see what we lack and don't lack in life. You lack nothing that is important. Your basic needs are met. Right at this moment you have enough.

So most middle-income people do not lack. But they do lust. They lust after things not only because of their desires for "more and better" but also because the incessant yapping of advertisers, telemarketers, movies, television, and magazines encourages lust. Here is that brainwashing thing again. The message is simple: You cannot and will not be satisfied with what you have. Ever.

Debating whether something is a want or a need is a lose-lose deal when the messages of consumption clobber us from every angle. *We could have bought the mattress that was highly rated in* Consumer Reports. *But after all, we are going to sleep every night for the rest of our lives. And that pillowtop-no-turn beauty is on sale. It makes sense to buy quality.* So we buy beyond our needs and beyond our wants.

Enough is what you have right now. Period. If you are in the middle class, you do not need any more. Period.

If you are faithful in little things, you will be entrusted with more. If not, you won't. If you learn to live on the amount of money you have now and enjoy the setting in which you find yourself, you will be content. And you will learn the secret to wealth: how to manage your finances when you have very little. This training will allow you to better manage your finances when you have more.

On the other hand, if you cannot manage on a little, you will not manage on a lot. Go back to the speech James Carter gave in chapter 2. If you are not content with a little, you will never be content with more.

You have enough right now. Your needs are met. Let's make sure you use that "enough" in such a way that it moves you into financial confidence and freedom.

WEALTH OR LIFESTYLE?

This is our life and our true desire:

START		Life		FINISH
BIRTH	Live Strong		Finish Well	DEATH

We all want to live strong and finish well. That means a growing faith, family, and career. This results in Right Relationships, which is what the kingdom of God is all about.

What is the major obstacle to living the life we want and developing those relationships? Money. What is the minor obstacle? Money. That is why Jesus talked about it so much. Without the correct use of money, our discipleship, marriages, families, and lives will be impaired. We will end up living okay and finishing mediocre.

START		Life		FINISH
BIRTH	Living Okay	Muddling Through	Finishing Mediocre	DEATH

You are making a choice every day as to which of those scenes is being played out in your life.

Do you want to *have* a life? Or do you want to *pretend* to have a life? Do you want to *be* wealthy, or do you want to *appear* to be wealthy? Huge difference. In *The Millionaire Mind*, Thomas Stanley writes that high income people are "income statement people" with no assets. Wealthy people are "balance sheet people" who have assets.[1]

Here's another way to put it: *Income and spending your income and/ or spending more than your income equals lifestyle.* People look wealthy but have no assets. They must look to the next paycheck. They are owned; they are not in charge of your life. However, they *look* good. And the culture's doctrine is, "If we look good, we will be good." Appearances lead to assumptions. When appearances and assumptions unite with comparison and competition, denial and delusion are not far behind.

Believe it or not, we have arrived at a formula:

$$A2 + C2 + D2 = FD^{10}$$

Appearance and Assumption plus Comparison and Competition
plus Denial and Delusion equal Financial Disaster to the Tenth Power

And another formula:

$$I + C2 - D = FW$$

Income plus Controlling Costs minus Debt equal Financial Wealth

You may not look wealthy, but you have assets. You do not have to look to the next paycheck; no one owns you. You are in charge of your life.

If you have come to believe that high income will give you a "lifestyle" and that your lifestyle is equivalent to your life, you have been deceived and are in serious trouble. If you are not already in pain, you are denying your symptoms. The pain will come very soon.

- lifestyle *or* wealth
- income *or* assets
- appearances and assumptions *or* reality

- a depreciating base and going back to the start *or* an appreciating base and heading toward the finish
- you are owned *or* you are free

NET WORTH IS IMPROPERLY DEFINED

Perhaps you have heard the term *net worth*. That is the current cultural expression for the amount of money one possesses. (All assets are given quantifiable worth in terms of dollars.) Books on finance say that knowing your net worth is very important. The authors then assume that you agree with them and launch into helping you discover your net *financial* worth. You see the trap? You are worth a good deal more than money or assets or whatever else the culture throws at you.

The experts tell you that your *worth* is associated with money. The CMC defers to people who have money or, once again, *appear* to have money. In other words, the CMC sees a "player" or a "somebody" in terms of their wealth or apparent wealth. This conveys mixed and wrong messages. If we have less money, we are subtly and unconsciously deemed worth-less. If we have money, we are worth more. The moneyed ones are the blessed of God. Nonsense. We all fall into this trap. We let the car, the address (heavens, we *must* have a custom home, not one of those awful tract homes), and the club determine our view of a person's *worth*.

I object to our "worth" being associated with money. "Wealth" deals with money; "worth" should not be associated with money. The more accurate term would be *net wealth,* not net worth.

We can see how this works practically on the Not Wealth/Net Wealth Scale on page 62. The scale has two sides: what you owe and what you own, *Not Wealth* and *Net Wealth.* Do you own more than you owe? Welcome to Net Wealth. Do you owe more than you own? Welcome to Not Wealth: Financial Purgatory.

You can live in the world of Net Wealth or in the world of Not

The Not Wealth / Net Wealth Scale

What You Owe   What You Own

Not Wealth   **Net Wealth**

Wealth. The scale is largely dependent on what you believe and how you act as a result of that belief. If you have been greedy, judgmental, lazy, fearful, or ignorant in the past, that can change. Today.

We all want to progress from the starting point in adulthood called Not Wealth to the finish line of adulthood called Net Wealth. Unfortunately, we are conflicted at every turn by things that work against our achieving the goal. I call this the Paralysis Circle. You can start anywhere you want on this circle. Inaccurate information will lead you back toward the starting gate (a.k.a. "investment advice from magazines"). The same fate awaits those who give in to fatigue, habit, time, and fear.

The Paralysis Circle

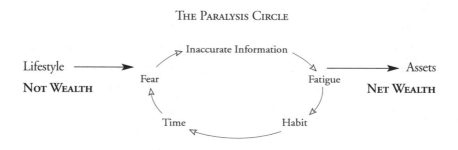

Lifestyle ———→

Not Wealth

Fear

Inaccurate Information

Fatigue   ———→ Assets

Net Wealth

Time   Habit

Now is the hour of your financial salvation, which comes from change. And why not? Change is not difficult. Perfection is difficult. Change is easy, as long as you understand that excellence will take some time. Perfection will not be experienced in your lifetime.

Change begins with a volitional decision, an act of your will. If you change and revert to former patterns, you have still changed. Recognize that you made a mistake and change back to the correct pattern. You might even want to pray about it. The Lord would welcome your words.

WE SHOULD ALL LIVE LIKE MOST MILLIONAIRES

We all have an image of what a millionaire's lifestyle should look like. Facts tell us that our image is wrong.[2]

I will use a few words that do *not* describe the actions of millionaires. They are bad words, and we should distance ourselves from them. Then I will use a few words that *do* describe the actions of millionaires. The words are not popular. They are good words. We must win back their integrity. (*A disclaimer:* There is usually a difference in the millionaire classification between those who earned and those who inherited their money. Inheritors, generally speaking, spend their money in ways that call attention to themselves. But most earners do the opposite, generally speaking. Let's live like earners.)

First the naughty words: *cheap* and *miserly*. Money is the end-all for cheap and miserly people. Relationships fall by the wayside as these folks go after their god. Quality never reigns supreme, only price. At a restaurant, these people always reach for their wallets a little too late or want to make sure they only pay the exact amount of their bill. *Must* we tip today? Cheap and miserly people are not generous. If they give at all, they will give to get something in the future. They have a long memory.

Now the good words: *frugal* and *thrifty*. Frugal and thrifty are to cheap and miserly what Billy Graham is to Bill Clinton: not even in the same league.

Most millionaires who have earned their fortunes are frugal and thrifty.

- They resole their shoes instead of buying new ones.
- They insist on quality, avoid fads, and pay a fair price.
- They shop for a long time before they make a sizable purchase.

- They have their furniture reupholstered instead of buying new.
- They live well below their means.
- They understand the future value of a dollar.
- Forty percent of them tithe.
- They have an economically productive household.
- They understand that they are not what they drive.
- They do not give economic outpatient care to their children.[3]

Shrewdness comes by imitation. We can do 75 percent of what millionaires do. So if we end up with only $750,000, would that be okay? (That doesn't seem like a lot to you? Check your current net-wealth statement. Now does it seem like a lot?)

Most millionaires, contrary to popular opinion, do not appear to be wealthy. They simply *are* wealthy.

Frugal Is Fun

You have been lied to and you bought the lie that frugal is bad. You think that frugal will diminish your life. You think that frugal means recycling dental floss. Frugal to you means *no fun!*

But frugal is good. The truth is good. Frugal means getting the best *value* out of each dollar spent. Your surrounding culture says Lexus ES 300. You decide on a Toyota Avalon XLS, which is nothing more than a roomier Lexus for less money. Frugal wealth is not impressed with image.

It would be most helpful if you would remold your mind from within so that you (and your spouse) will determine what gives the most bang for your buck—and more important, the greatest joy. Hobbies, for instance, can be both frugal and fun. Some hobbies are productive and some are nonproductive. Some hobbies provide entertainment and creative diversion but are very expensive and have no economic benefit. My experience with sports cars, golf, skiing, shopping, and boating have led me to this painfully expensive knowledge: The Fab Five are black holes that pillage your wallet and laugh while they are doing it!

But some hobbies provide entertainment and creative diversion as well as an economic benefit. Finding this kind of hobby is crucial. A productive hobby puts you firmly on the Net Wealth side of the scale (or at least it begins to move you in that direction). For the time being, until we are out of Devastating Debt, we will give up all of the Fab Five hobbies. We will institute new ones.

You say, "What now? I suppose we have to make lanyards?"

Well, you could, but only if you really enjoyed that kind of activity.

What do you enjoy doing? Do you like the outdoors? How about volunteering to be an assistant coach or statistician for your daughter's soccer team? How about hiking some of the beautiful parks in your area? Do you like color? Why not redecorate your house on a shoestring and with a paintbrush? Why not learn to apply architectural principles to your lawn and garden by adding flowers and cutting and edging the lawn? Why not learn to take care of the maintenance of your home and insulate the windows, doors, and cracks around the house? Do you like to work with your hands? Why not learn to build rustic furniture? Why not learn strength training at home? If you're married, why not kick up your sex life a notch?

You do not have to give up anything to start moving toward assets and Net Wealth. You will simply have to add so many new things to your life that you will not be able to practice old things until you have understood money. You will be moving toward the finish instead of continuously starting over.

STEPS TOWARD SHREWD

- Life is lived on the inside: The kingdom of God is within you. You may believe this, but your actions probably don't always reflect that belief.

- More money will not bring contentment.
- Ask yourself, What do I lack?
- Do you want wealth or a lifestyle of wealth?
- The Not Wealth/Net Wealth Scale has two sides: What you own and what you owe. You want to move away from Not Wealth and toward Net Wealth!
- Most millionaires who have earned their fortunes are frugal and thrifty. We should all live like them.
- Frugal can be fun; it means getting the best value out of every dollar spent.

5

True Riches

J esus stated repeatedly that there was more to life than money. There was a better life than the life money could buy. It was available to all and the cost could not be counted in dollars.

Jesus wants us to have a full life. That life has to do with value. Part of a valued life is money—an important part, but not the most essential part. Truly rich is different than financially wealthy. Truly rich means that you have great relationships. Pastor Bruce Larsen once said, "The kingdom of God is the kingdom of right relationships." He could not be more correct. Growing relationships with the Lord, others, yourself, and your work, make life enjoyable. Life works when relationships are good. Life does not work when relationships are not good.

I do not believe middle-class people have money problems that lead to relationship problems. I believe they have relationship problems that lead to money problems.

How many of us have let people borrow money and then watched how the relationship dissolved because they could not or would not pay it back? Notice how your adolescent does a great sulk job if he or she cannot get the shoes that are the hottest thing. I wonder where the phrase "the silent treatment" came from.

I can see from experience how my own financial selfishness compounded relationship problems in my marriage, family, and work. I've learned that if I spend the rest of the money in the checking account to meet my own needs without considering the needs of other family members, I may have something I wanted, but I may also have distressed the rest of the family.

Good relationships lead to good life. No matter the circumstances, if relationships are good, life is worth living. I bet you can guess what bad relationships lead to. Whether you're married or single, bad relationships lead to the misuse of money. The misuse of money usually means self-serving spending, Devastating Debt, and the neglect of our financial responsibility toward the Lord.

Getting on the Same Page

It is common knowledge that many marriages are in trouble because of money issues. It is my opinion that this common knowledge is wrong. Many marriages slide into relationship and communication standoffs. Patterns develop that result in limited, if any, communication about certain issues. Money is one of those issues. Satisfactory compromises may not be reached in a marriage, but money will still be spent. The result is constant *flustration*—being flustered and frustrated at the same time.

Those who argue about money say, "If we have enough money, we will enjoy our marriage. If we are not enjoying our marriage, more money is the answer. If we could just get out of debt… If we could just afford a decent vacation… If we could just afford to send our kids to a different school…" While it appears that people argue over money, they are really reminding themselves that:

    a. they do not know how to communicate and reach compromises,

    b. they do not understand what they are up against,

    c. they do not have a coherent means of attack to put money in its proper place, or

    d. all of the above.

"None of the above" is not an option. Money issues are symptoms of larger relational problems. We're in the habit of attacking symptoms, but not the cause. We're like doctors dealing with the symptoms of cancer, but not the disease itself.

If the purpose of money is to build relationships, and marriage is one of the prime relationships, then using money to build your marriage relationship makes sense. If you do not have any money, you must build the relationship in order to get some. By working together on your finances, you will out-think and outperform couples who are not working together on their finances. If you do not build your relationship, the money will not come.

Any problem in marriage can be solved if the relationship is good. Any problem will grow in magnitude if the relationship is not good. A good relationship means that we are open and honest with each other, constantly trying to "out-serve" each other (no, not tennis), listen to each other, and meet each other's needs. A good relationship involves *honesty* and *support*.

Now there is a secret to this serving each other: Does your spouse see what you do for him or her as service, or do you merely *believe* that you are serving your spouse whether or not he or she perceives it? Perception is everything.

I know one man, a student of golf, who surprised his wife on her fortieth birthday with a brand new set of golf clubs. He said, "After you take a few lessons, we can play together once in a while." To my knowledge, the golf clubs were never touched. He perceived that he was serving her. That perception did not pass the reality test.

If we do the honesty/support thing, we will probably be okay with money. It doesn't mean we will be rich, just content. Contentment is a great experience.

A not-good relationship means that we are not open and honest with each other, that we are constantly trying to "out-get" the other and talk about meeting our needs ahead of those of our spouse. If that is the case, we will probably not be okay with money. It doesn't mean we will be rich, just discontent. Discontentment is not a good experience. Most arguments will then center on money. It *appears* that money is the culprit. The poor relationship is the real culprit.

This does not mean that good relationships never have arguments or tension. But honesty and support help you work through the difficulties. A house divided against itself cannot stand. Nowhere is this truer than in relationships and with money.

Economic wars are the usual result of self-centeredness replacing communication. Let me give you an example of this. Several years ago I wanted a dog. The kids wanted a dog. Margie wasn't quite ready for a dog. One Saturday during the fall the kids and I went for a "ride" and came home with a golden retriever puppy.

"Hi, hon! Would you like to meet Deacon?"

The glacial age descended on our home. Margie stared me in the eye as she patted the cute little thing. Then she announced, "I am going shopping."

Margie spent $378 on new clothes. When she came home, she asked with that same stare if I liked her new clothes. Oh boy, did I ever like her new clothes!

My action of buying Deacon had set off a war. Deacon wasn't in the house one day, and he had cost us almost $600!

Research suggests that there is a huge correlation between divorce and nonwealth. If you have one, it is likely you will have the other. Divorce is painful. It is also costly; especially if you are in the middle class.

A friend recently told the story of a study done with thirty Christian men who retired at the age of fifty-five with a net wealth of at least $5 million. Two years later, twenty-seven (90 percent) were divorced. They had money, but no matter how you slice it, if they did not work on their marriages, they were not truly rich.

Likewise there is a correlation between marriage and wealth. If you have one, it is much easier to acquire the other. Spouses together can achieve wealth. What do great relationships have to do with becoming wealthy? Everything! By far the most important financial step we can take is being on the same page with our spouse.

Okay, let's say that you are the only CMCer not on the same page with your spouse. (Fat chance that you are the only one.) Do not feel guilty. Instead, feel *thirsty.* You are missing something. Find the ingredients that quench your relational thirst.

I once had to refer a couple I was supervising to a psychologist who specialized in marriage problems. I was concerned about this couple and asked the psychologist if he was concerned about their future in ministry. He smiled at my naiveté and answered, "Most good marriages of today have been the bad marriages of yesterday." It was true. After a few months of good, honest counseling, the couple was healthier, and they flourished in ministry for years after that.

If one partner is dominant, he or she may be able to "out-talk" the other partner and win the battle. He or she will have the partner's head. But the dominant one will lose the war because the couple is *not* on the same page. He or she will not have the partner's heart. If that is the case, money will become a "get-even" tool.

Paul Tournier has said that everyone has a deep need to be heard and understood. That is the same for every couple: Each person needs to have his or her needs understood and appreciated, not necessarily met, by the other. Life is difficult. We need to be able to count on each other to make this work.

As I was writing this book, a phrase kept appearing over and over again in the manuscript: "the two of us." It meant that Margie and I had talked through our financial plans. Whether they were of a simple or crisis nature, we talked them through. The two of us came to conclusions. The two of us implemented the decisions. The two of us have reaped the rewards. Our household is wealthy today for one reason and one reason alone: Margie and I have been on the same page for 90 percent of our marriage.

We have had to work through a few things. We had both been burned by life. We made bad mistakes. But we did not let them get in the way.

We have learned and we have lived life. We have enjoyed life far beyond what we had thought was possible. We have been great parents and wretched parents. We know what it is to be a great friend and a poor friend. We have had great friends and false friends. We have been rich and we have been poor. We have been around the block a time or two. But we are still on the same page.

Without a spiritual base, rich is all about money: getting it and keeping it. The only thing that being rich gives you is money. Life is stillborn. With a spiritual base you have a foundation of truth upon which you can add wealth.

Win/Win or No Deal

My mom and dad were divorced after forty years of marriage. I am convinced to this day that they deeply loved each other. But Mom loved Dad on her terms, not his. Dad loved Mom on his terms, not hers. Their marriage collapsed. Their three sons were devastated by the breakup. We knew there were problems, but we never thought they would lead to divorce. We handled it in different ways, but one of the major contributions to our lives (i.e., their marriage) was no longer there for us.

To arrive at authentic win/win situations, no one must lose. If a compromise is to be attained, both parties must give equally, it must literally be Win/Win or No Deal.[1] What happens if you spend a weekend on an issue, and it cannot be resolved? A weekend? A lousy weekend? Shoot, you have no idea what difficult resolutions are all about if you think a weekend can solve some problems. But here is the answer: You just keep talking and talking and talking until you get new insights and turn it into win/win.

For example: One year Margie and I found ourselves in semiserious financial yogurt. After a little research I determined the situation could be corrected if we did not eat out for the next three months and I gave up golf. We would be fine. I did not really mind giving up golf; it had given up on me the first year I played it. Besides, I was now into gardening.

Can you imagine how Margie's part of that "solution" would have been perceived from her point of view? At that time she was the primary caregiver with two small children. Eating out meant getting out—going someplace where someone else actually prepared the food, served the food, cleaned the table, served coffee, and did the dishes. In the summer it also meant air conditioning. My answer for rescuing us from our financial dilemma could end up causing her real pain.

So when I stated that restaurants were verboten for three months, I also made an offer to help her over that very substantial hurdle. The kids were now old enough to graduate from not only clearing the table but to doing the dishes as well. Wow! What fun! My job would be to cook meals several times a week and do a little of the grocery shopping. In addition, we would do one fun thing for each person at the end of the three months. My job also was to help the family have more life with less money.

Everyone got into it. After a little initial "adjusting," things went well until we hit the midpoint mark and we needed to do some more adjusting. But we made it through the tough times with our family and pocketbook intact. We look back now and recognize that we did not have to "give up" anything. We added things to our lives and had more life for less money.

Date Nights and Other Ways to Fall Back in Love

Dating patterns are different today than they used to be. Many people stop dating after kids enter the family scene. Maybe the couple were DINKs (Dual Income, No Kids) before children, and money was no problem. Now one person wants to stay at home and the couple become SIWKs (Single Income with Kids).

Many people come to a marriage without understanding the "roots" of the other person. They might feel no need to talk about financial history in early marriage. Kids, as usual, are the great levelers of life and marriage—often, it is their arrival that stimulates financial discussion.

One of the best things you can do to get on the same page with your spouse—and stay there—is to have regular date nights. The following is a basic pattern; I have no doubt that you can come up with better ideas.

The idea is to talk, learn, and grow. If one of you can out-talk the other, I have a three-point sermon for you: (1) shut up; (2) listen up; and (3) lighten up.

First week. Okay, here are the rules: Restaurant with carpet, tablecloths, linen napkins, servers, and good food. Prepare to tip 20 percent—you will be back next week, and you will want the restaurant to greet you with open arms. No mall, movie, sporting event, or concert after dinner. Just the two of you. Do not try to bring little Billy along. Your goal: Each person must share his or her personal/family financial histories during dinner. One person shares; the other person takes notes. Then switch. (Guys, bring your own paper, listen carefully, take notes. Trust me on this. You do *not* want to trust your memory.)

What was money like in your house growing up? Was there too much, too little? Was it talked about, was it worshiped, was it feared, was it squandered, was it hoarded? Listen closely, one half of yourself is speaking, and the words may help you understand the strategies your other half is employing in your marriage. Independent of your spouse's history, his or her actions may make no sense to you. But with the history, understanding may come. And therefore a legitimate strategy.

Second week. Same or better restaurant. Still tip 20 percent. Now each of you will recount the personal/family financial history of your spouse.

Third week. The List of Favorites, the number one wealth building tool. The List of Favorites is the most important tool you can develop for enjoying more life with less money. I learned this at a Bill Gothard seminar in the early seventies and still practice it. Write long Lists of Favorites—your favorite ice cream, color, flower, pizza, fast food, sport, pet, movie, magazine, day activity, weekend destination, vacation, and so on.

If our golfer friend in a previous illustration had a list of his wife's favorites, he would not have spent several hundred dollars on a mistake that had an emotional cost as well.

I like to put the List of Favorites into action. This is how it worked when we were a young family. Margie loves See's Candies, not Russell Stover. She likes white daisies, not yellow daisies. One day I was feeling really good and bought *both* See's Candies and white daisies. I drove into the garage but decided that this was too special an event. I went around to the front door and rang the bell. Margie came to the door, saw me with my smile, the candy, and the flowers. She began to cry. Something I had not expected. I said, "Margie, what's wrong?" She replied, "Oh, Matt got in a fight at school today. Jodi has the flu and is throwing up. And now you come home drunk!"

Here are the three pillars of fun with which to build your relationship with your spouse:

1. *Keep on falling in love with each other.* Sure you have droughts. Sure you get in ruts. But you do fun things together and you understand one another. For a long period of time.

   Remember that wealth and divorce are related—divorce is a disaster that makes it difficult to become wealthy. Wealth and health are also related—if you are healthy, you are more likely to become wealthy. If a couple is not getting along, there is a greater risk of one of them becoming sick, and therefore more likely to move toward Not Wealth. And finally, wealth and age are related. On average, older Americans who have not allowed themselves to be deceived are very well off. They understand reality. They have invested in their relationships.

2. *Repeat pillar 1 until you have it mastered.*

3. *Increase sexual activity with your spouse.* If one of you is too tired or not enjoying it, get some help. It is my opinion that most evening "headaches" are the result of inadequate intimacy in the relationship. Therefore, physical intimacy is not welcome until

emotional intimacy is restored. (See pillars 1 and 2 above.)

Mark Kahler, my physician in Overland Park, Kansas, said the two best stress relievers in the world are exercise and sex.

Enough said.

After you and your spouse are on the same page, you should have a CTA (Clear the Air) talk with your children. Decide together with your spouse how you will present this talk. It should bring your kids up to speed on the family finances and the need to have more life with less money. Let them know that you are really looking for their ideas to make it happen. And if they need more money, they can always figure out creative ways to earn it *outside* the family.

Truly Rich in Every Part of Life

This final section is of great importance. It is controversial but very crucial for a number of readers. I include it because the purpose of this book is to give people hope.

If you love Jesus, your spouse, and your family but still find yourself sabotaging your relationships, something is very wrong. You may have tried every spiritual route available, such as Bible studies, different worship experiences, Promise Keepers/Women of Faith, and so on. You may feel guilty, shamed, anxious, fearful, and perhaps mad. You may wake up at three o'clock every morning with mild panic coursing through your body, limiting further rest. You may feel uptight or a little sad all day and be tempted to think that you are a poor disciple not walking the talk. You need help.

In 1996 at the age of fifty-four, I was diagnosed with adult attention deficit hyperactivity disorder. I had listened to a tape by Dr. James Dobson of Focus on the Family on ADHD. Of the twenty symptoms of this disorder, I had nineteen. Since that time I have taken a drug that has greatly improved my quality of life. It was like going from a black-and-white life to a life of vivid color. I did not lose any of my enthusiasm or creativity. I did lose impulsiveness, my lack of concentration, and my lack of ability to focus or sit still for more than ten minutes.

Life was better, much better, but I was still dealing with anxiety. I also still had an unexplainable sadness that seemed to conflict with the spiritual fruit of joy. I was determined to correct this deficiency in my spiritual life. Books, fasting, retreats, confession, small groups, discipling by wonderful men of God, counseling—you name it, I was game for it.

One day I was telling my office partner about this dilemma. She and her husband are longtime friends. She also happens to be a marriage and family therapist. She said, "You are talking about something that could be physiological, not spiritual or psychological."

I was willing to listen and try anything if it meant I could love and enjoy Jesus more, as well as my family and those around me. Mary sent me to a friend. That physician determined that I had a mixed anxiety/depressive disorder and prescribed an antidepressant, Paxil.

Within a few weeks my anxiety disappeared as did most of my sadness. Life was cranked up another notch. Thank you, Lord! I started living life in a new way. One day my daughter was riding in the car with Margie, and out of the blue she said, "Mom, I *love* Paxil!" She is not on it, I am! I realized how much my relationships had changed for the better.

Obviously, I share this with a little nervousness. I do not mean to imply that my solution is your solution, nor will medicine replace spiritual exercise and discipline. Not everyone needs to go this route. But if you or your spouse recognize that pattern, I urge you to talk to your physician. He will be able to guide you through the proper procedures to get a correct diagnosis.

If you're still hesitant about this, let me give you an example: Let's say that Sam has diabetes; his pancreas is not secreting enough insulin. One day his doctor introduces him to the insulin he is missing. Immediately his life improves. Is Sam a bad fellow for taking insulin and not trusting

God for healing? Nearly all of us would say, "No way!" If your child steps on a rusty nail, would you say no to a tetanus shot? If your dad had an infected wound, would you counsel against penicillin?

If you are relationally paralyzed by defeating behavior, I urge you to pray and seek help. Your life, your discipleship, and your true riches could be at stake.

RIGHT RELATIONSHIPS

If you agree that the kingdom of God is the kingdom of Right Relationships and you live in light of that knowledge, you will do well and so will your relationships. If you do not agree, life will trap you, squeeze you, defeat you, and smile at you the whole way. You are choosing someone else's plan. That would not be shrewd.

Relationships can hinder us from overcoming most of life's difficulties, or they can help us overcome them. When you have true riches, you feel as if you are part of a larger picture. You are well connected with people. You love and are loved. You are aware of the Lord's work in your life and are participating in that work. If you are married, you have a good marriage. If you are single, you have a good single life. If you have children, they are growing in the Lord and have a good relationship with you…most of the time. You enjoy your work and are involved in a community of faith. When you realize relationships are what life is all about and you have those relationships, you are truly rich.

STEPS TOWARD SHREWD

- The kingdom of God is the kingdom of Right Relationships.
- If you do not have Right Relationships, you will not be content. Right Relationships bring contentment, and that is being truly rich!

- Being on the same page with your spouse is essential to both true riches and financial wealth.
- Win/Win or No Deal is the way to Right Relationships.
- If you are relationally paralyzed, look for the source; it probably is *not* money.

Part
Two

Making It Work

6

Playing to Win

Have you ever surfed or body surfed? Every beginner has difficulty learning to read the waves—it is something only experience can teach. Surf rookies are often roughly introduced to the ocean floor. But each time the wave wins a round, the would-be surfer *comes up laughing!* It is fun in a painful sort of way; you know you'll be a master surfer someday. No one in their right mind takes surfing seriously (except for a few "dudes," of course). Besides, those learning incidents make great stories over a ginger ale: "Man, I really bought it when this three-hundred-foot wave came out of nowhere."

The best way to master money is to treat it as if you are learning to surf: Do not take it too seriously. Many people have learned to become financially wealthy on a small salary. All the little people who developed assets had one thing in common: They made a *game* of it, a game they played to win. As in any learning phase there is the beginning phase in which we think, *Hey, this is easy. I should master it quickly.* This is followed by the reality phase, *Whoa! This is a little trickier than it looks.* Finally, the last phase when we are able to compete with the best. We learned the secret: we mastered the little things and applied them appropriately.

Most people like to play games if they have a reasonable chance of winning, if they understand the rules and believe the rules are fair, and if they like the game. So here are the rules of our financial game: (1) you have to know what your opponents are doing, and you have to develop an effective counterstrategy, and (2) you have to learn and apply KISMIF (Keep It Simple, Make It Fun).

We are going to go from coma to consciousness, from awareness to alertness and competence. If the leap could be made from coma to consciousness overnight, we would all breathe more easily and live happily ever after. But in the lingo of the surfer, you have to bite the floor a few times to learn what is really real. Attaining the level of Financial Alertness may take some doing on your part. How long? It depends on your native ability and where you are starting. If you are an above-average person and diligently apply the principles in this book, you may get there in one hundred days. If you are an average person and use the principles sporadically, it will take longer. Either way you need a game plan. As all the rest of us "little people" discovered, you can't afford a "nice try." This is a game to win.

THE GAME AND THE GAME PLAN

You as a middle-class Christian are choosing your own participation in the game. You are working one of two plans: (1) your conscious plan, or (2) the culture's conscious plan.

So with or without your permission, you are in this game; winner takes all. The cultural game plan is for you to have a phenomenal front-door income (lots of money coming in) with an unlocked, wide-open back door (lots of money going out). They want you to earn, earn, earn so you can buy, buy, buy. The goal of your opponents is to blind you and bind you; blind you to true riches and bind you in financial chains. Their tactic is confusion: too much coming at you too fast for you to make good judgments. When that happens, they win. Hands down, no contest.

Our counterstrategy is trustworthy, accurate information: What is really going down, and how can we turn the tables? We turn the tables by realizing we have families to feed, and we are not responsible for feeding the families of sales machines. In other words, we can *change the rules!* How much fun is that? In the middle of the game, we can change the way the game is played so that it is played in our favor. And we don't have to ask our opponents if it is okay with them. We just do it!

Of course our opponents will cry, "Foul, not fair. After all, this is a consumer-based economy!" Ha, sounds fun already, doesn't it? Make 'em whine. Believe me, it doesn't get any better than beating the culture at its own game. We, the CMC, will take over the game and change one person and one family at a time. But there is so much to learn and so little time for application. Can we really make it work? Let me give you a picture of successful corporate change over a very short amount of time.

In 1970 the United States made the world's "finest" automobiles. Shoot, the little Japanese import, the Toyota Corolla or whatever it was called, was so bad that the brake pedal actually bent if the driver exerted too much pressure on it! Of course, American cars really were not meant to live a long life: Fifty thousand miles meant that it was time to get a new one. And if they ate gas for a living, broke often, and were generally unsafe, well, that was too bad.

Fast-forward ten years. In 1980 the U.S. auto industry began buying Toyotas and taking them apart to learn why those little cars were so superior to GM, Ford, and Chrysler. It turned out they had stronger brake pedals and stronger everything else. They were on a gas diet, broke seldom, and became safer and safer. They also lasted a long time. The American public couldn't get enough of them.

That finally caught the attention of the Big Three. American cars are now beginning to catch up; that is, the quality gap is still there, but it is no longer as wide. Why have American cars made such gigantic improvements in the last twenty years? Toyota changed the rules of the game (without asking Detroit's permission) and forced Americans to try harder. A good deal for consumers who want a vehicle that can last 200,000 miles.

If it can work in that big picture, I know it can work in our little picture. So let the game begin.

Changing the Game Plan

The purpose of this game is to help us move to the highest category of being Financially Alert. Our goal is Financial Alertness and contentment. But we are way behind in today's game (read: lots of Devastating Debt), have always been defeated in the past (read: lots of Devastating Debt), and have little confidence that things can turn around.

We need an illustration here. Is there a story, say from sports, that could help us understand that even though we are not favored we can still win? Glad you asked.

The 2001 St. Louis Rams had the best offense the football world has ever seen. They were the first team to score five hundred points or more in three consecutive seasons. Their opponents in the Super Bowl were the New England Patriots. The Patriots were two-touchdown underdogs. In normal language that means the game did not really need to be played because the Patriots were on the not-able-to-perform list.

There was a reason for this. The Patriots had played the Rams earlier in the season. They gave the Rams a great game. Only lost by a touchdown. Held the Rams to twenty-four points instead of their average thirty-eight. A moral victory. The Patriots kept it close by blitzing everyone and the kitchen sink. (Okay all you nonfootball fans, listen up: Blitzing means that a lot of players run at and try to hurt, er, tackle the quarterback. Football fans love it when the blitzers get him but are sad [well, at least a little] if he is hurt.) Rams quarterback Kurt Warner was under constant pressure.

Super Bowl preparation for the Rams was intense. Imagine the harried defensive coaches of the Rams. They studied films. They noticed which Patriot blitzed when and from where. The Rams offense had been exposed. Now they were going to prepare a game plan that would take out the threat of that blitzing defense. They prepared, practiced, preached, screamed, and drilled until each and every offensive player knew what to do in each and every situation where the Patriots could blitz. Ha! The Invincible Machine meets normal humans. No contest.

Final score: Patriots 20, Rams 17. Contest.

Why? The Patriots changed; they did *not* blitz. They saw what they did in the past. It didn't work. They had no intention of playing the game to not *lose;* they were playing the game to *win.* They changed the game plan. Did something different. No blitzing. They dropped back in coverage, five, six, sometimes seven defensive backs. The Rams had prepared for the *wrong* game plan. The Patriots forged a different plan and won. They were shrewd. The Rams were not. The Patriots had a better game plan. They saw truth in the future and put it into practice—and won. The Rams saw truth in the past, put it into practice, and lost.

When we change the rules of our financial game and play to win, we will enter the ranks of the Financially Alert. With proper strategies, you can reach the following goals according to your age. (This is more art than science.)

- In your twenties: pay off any kind of debt, discover a decent career, plan an appropriate lifestyle, learn to do little things excellently.
- In your thirties: continue the above, buy a home with a large down payment, start and enjoy a family.
- In your forties: continue the above, pay off the home, use the former mortgage payment to fund your children's educations.
- In your fifties: continue the above (except you no longer have a mortgage or education payments…don't you miss them?), use your former payments to fund your retirement account.
- In your sixties: continue the above until you can retire (switch to God's next call on your life).
- In your seventies: smile.
- In your eighties: smile some more.

You can reach these goals by practicing the six rock-solid, earthquake-proof principles of middle-class financial wealth:

1. generosity
2. an appropriate lifestyle
3. an owned house and automobile(s) free and clear of all debt
4. appropriate insurance
   a. life
   b. house
   c. auto
   d. health
   e. disability
   f. long-term care
   g. perhaps an umbrella policy for liability
5. paid-for education for your children
6. an appropriate accumulation of funds for retirement

Getting the final game plan in place could take about nine months. It takes that long because the vagaries of life do not appear on a scheduled basis. You will have to adjust, readjust, fail, fail, and fail once again until you finally get it. Let's remember the surfing illustration. A lot of bumps and bruises, but the result of riding one excellent wave makes you a surfer for life. You only need one excellent financial score, and you will be alert for life. But you have made progress today. Wait until you see the really big money savers among all the little things you have surrounding you.

The Shrewd Christian game plan has two parts: (1) a decent income, and (2) a locked and guarded back door and controlled spending, founded on the SOE (Save on Everything) and the GVE (Get Value for Everything) strategies.

The overarching truth is: The less you spend, the more you have. So Save on Everything and Get Value for Everything. Do it for a long period of time. You're on your way to winning the game.

SAVE ON EVERYTHING

A friend of mine, Rabbi Howard Hirsch, likes to tell the story of the Jewish grandpa talking with his grandson to point out stereotypes.

"Grandpa, why did God make Gentiles?"

Grandpa thought a moment and replied, "Well, someone had to pay retail."

Sales happen in places where you spend money. You may have saved 75 percent, but you still are out the 25 percent (MONEY!) that the item cost you. Therefore, you have less money now than you did before you bought something and "saved" money. Let me give you an example.

You are at the mall picking up candy for your spousal unit. A thought pops into your head: *The papers keep saying that consumers will lead us out of the recession. Consumers have a patriotic duty to move this country out of a recession!* Silly how little thoughts like that turn up at odd moments—usually when you are in places where people are willing and able to take your money.

On the way out to your car, you just happen to wander through the men's section of Nordstrom's. They are known for quality, service, tuxedoed musicians performing on the main floor, and, of course, high prices.

As you wander through the store, you see a rack of sports coats marked "SALE." You decide to take a look. You find one you really like! You look at the price. *Oh, this is too good to be true!* Today only, the $400 sports coat is on sale for $200. Well it is still a little pricey. But then, as if by magic, a sales "associate" (a.k.a. "machine") approaches you and says in her classic way, "That coat is my *personal* favorite! I just love it. Here, let me help you try it on...a perfect fit. You look *soooo* good in it. We don't even need to make any alterations—that will save you a bundle. And did you know that this is the last day of the sale and you can take an additional 50 percent off the sale price?"

"Golly, do you mean that this $400 coat can be had for $100?"

"Will that be Visa or MasterCard?"

Did you save anything? Not one dime! You spent $100. It gets worse! You didn't ask yourself if you *needed* a sports coat. You didn't even ask yourself if you *lacked* a sports coat. The result is that you bought a depreciating item and filled your closet with a coat you didn't need. And all because the blatant messages bombarding you every day have made you susceptible to impulse buying. (What do you think you could get for that coat at a garage sale tomorrow even if the price tag is still on it?)

Repeat after me: *I cannot save money by spending money. I cannot save money by spending money. I cannot save money by spending money. Everyone is after my money.*

So here is our plan. *SOE: Save on Everything.* It is simple and it is possible.

Get Value for Everything

A young couple from Denver Seminary recently came to my office to talk about finances. They were doing great for their situation but felt they were not doing enough. Cindy stated that she had given up her job, was staying at home as a Residential CEO (see chapter 10), and could prove that she and her husband, Steve, were ahead financially. They had diligently tracked every expenditure for seven months. We met as a kind of mid-course checkup/correction.

One of their concerns centered on school debt. They had other assets, so I was not too worried about the debt that had accumulated. We bantered back and forth for a while, then Steve said something that startled me: "We don't eat out that often." I was startled because I had the record of expenses in front of me. In the first fifteen days, they had eaten out thirteen times!

I remarked that the evidence seemed to contradict his statement. He amended his words by saying, "It doesn't *feel* like we eat out that often."

They obviously thought I would scold them for being in tough financial shape and "wasting" money by eating at restaurants. Instead I asked the question, "Did you get *value* for eating out as often as you did? Or was it an impromptu decision based on immediate hunger?" They did not know how to answer that question. I continued by asking them to look at the average amount they had spent eating out over the last seven months. After that they needed to decide whether they could spend that money in a more productive way. For example, instead of eating nine fast-food meals, could they save their money for two date nights at decent restaurants?

The two key questions to ask before you spend money are: (1) does it build relationships? and (2) does it add to the Net Wealth side of the scale?

You may say, "If we just use our money to build relationships, we may never build Net Wealth!" The response is obvious: If you only spend money on relationships and ignore Net Wealth, there will come a day when the Not Wealth side of the scale will *impinge* on the relationships. Getting Value for Everything means keeping both relationships and Net Wealth in mind.

I do not know your life situation; therefore, I cannot give you detailed advice about how to spend your money. Only you can determine that. But a great way to start is to evaluate whether you are getting your money's worth. After you eat out, are you glad or sad? Was this a good time or a routine time? If it had little or no value, why continue? Why not replace it with something better?

LITTLE THINGS MEAN A LOT

I recently ranch-sat at a beautiful home about five miles north of Buena Vista, Colorado. What could go wrong in such a pleasing environment? Well, everything seemed to be going well—I was tending a few animals, enjoying the beauty of the place, fishing, eating, writing—talk about getting good value!—until about 2:30 one morning.

My host had carefully, and thankfully, positioned a hot tub on the deck facing the Collegiate Range. It was a dark night. With the outside and most of the inside lights off, I could see the profile of the mountains. It was early evening and the first few stars were gathering. It was a perfect opportunity for warm watery relaxation.

I went outside to get the tub going and was heading back inside to change when I discovered I was locked out. It was at this point that I realized again how much little things mean.

For example, when the French door deadbolt is unlatched, a person can easily move outside. Returning inside, however, requires that both the deadbolt *and* the handle lock are released. That little thing in the handle of the French door was in the vertical position. The little thing in the handle needed to be in the horizontal position. It was a small thing, but it meant I was locked out of the ranch house. Have I mentioned that this happened on a crisp December night? Because I didn't know about the little door handle lock, I had to break a window to get back into the house! A mess, a waste of time and energy, and a humbling experience. Little things mean a lot.

Somehow a lot of people forget that little things mean a lot when it comes to money. Their brain is divorced from reality. Money means getting a lot "right now." So some play the lottery; the rest play the stock market—both looking for that one score. But over a period of time, a *little* and a *lot* connect. Most people are not visited by the financial monster named "disaster." Most people do not experience a house fire, the physical pain of a hit-and-run accident, or a life-threatening medical emergency that requires surgery and extended recovery. Yet the AARP states that "there is a 4 in 10 chance that an American will be poor at some time in his or her life after the age of 60.... The remarkable economic growth we have experienced is not enough to provide true economic security for the majority of Americans over 50."[1]

For a middle-class person to become financially secure, he or she must understand that little amounts of money are the basis for wealth. That sounds too unrealistic. People argue that we should go after large amounts of money; small amounts take too long to grow.

So the action plan is to get more money? Well, not exactly. The action plan is to decide how to better use your resources. If you are married, your primary resources are your spouse and your family. As they come to understand the plan and contribute ideas, you will watch true riches come alive before your eyes. The Shrewd Christian game plan assumes that if you are married you are on the same page with your spouse. The SC game plan also assumes that if you are single, you have good, supportive relationships.

The plan then deals with the resource of current money. The idea is to create little profit pockets from what we earn, become more generous, pay off debt, and never go back to being controlled by money. In other words, savings from goods and services are not channeled back into lifestyle (Not Wealth) but are used to build assets (Net Wealth).

The road that leads to Financial Confidence begins with Financial Competence in little things. It is a long journey. But if we choose Financial Competence and master *all* the little things, we will be content at the end of the road.

Now something practical. Go to the thermostat. Depending on what season it is, raise or lower the temperature setting by two degrees. Congratulations, you are on the road to wealth!

Do not scoff! Each degree of adjustment produces a 3 percent reduction in your heating/cooling bill. A little thing. Little things mean a lot. The paved highway to financial wealth is laid with one small brick at a time. You will be surprised and delighted when you see how easily the highway can be built and how much you can get done in a short period of time.

So Save on Everything and Get Value for Everything. If you're feeling discouraged because you don't have much money to begin with, remember that starting with less always leads to more because we *must* pay attention when we have less. You're already ahead of the game.

True Truths of the Game

As you move toward saving on everything and getting value for everything, the lies of the Bad Shepherds will be replaced with *true truths*. Here are some of those truths to keep in mind:

1. You *cannot* become wealthy by spending unnecessarily.
2. You *cannot* become wealthy by throwing money away.
3. You *cannot* become wealthy by supporting a lifestyle.
4. You *can* become wealthy by not spending unnecessarily.
5. You *can* become wealthy by not throwing money away.
6. You *can* become wealthy by not supporting a lifestyle.

You want to stay married to the positive corollaries and divorce the negative ones. In this case, divorce is perfectly biblical.

Steps Toward Shrewd

- You have to know the game plan of the culture and have an effective counterstrategy.
- KISMIF—Keep It Simple, Make It Fun is your way to wealth.
- SOE—Save on Everything! You cannot save money by spending money.
- GVE—Get Value for Everything.
- Remember that little things mean a lot: $LT + E(T) + A^2 = L$ *(Little Things done Excellently over Time and Applied Appropriately add up to Lots!)*

7

Paying Attention or Pain and Tension?

One day a few years ago I told Margie that I had found the secret to life.

Margie: "Okay, Neil, what is your secret this time?"

I was so excited about my discovery that I ignored her patronizing tone. I shared the secret.

Margie looked interested but puzzled. Finally she said, "Well, I think that those things could be part of a secret to life, but I am not sure they fit completely."

Now I had only said *one* thing. Margie heard "things." I had a clue with which I could work to solve the mystery of why she was not falling over at my brilliance.

"Margie, what did you hear me say is the secret to life?"

"Neil, you said that the secret to life is pain and tension."

"No, hon, I said that the secret to life is paying attention."

As Margie and I speak at different events, we often use that illustration. Many times people believe they are hearing something correctly, but they are misunderstanding the real point.

My goal in this chapter is to help you understand that *shrewdness comes by paying attention.* No secret. You must have correct information and know how to apply that information. Not exactly like performing brain surgery. Paying attention means being aware of the little things, planning ahead, and keeping track of where your money is going. It means using your head and a relatively brief amount of time every week to relieve pain and tension in your life.

The Magic 80

"Time. That is the problem. I don't have enough of it. I am too tired from my job, my kids, and church. I will never have time to put the program into place."

People are exhausted from work. Exhaustion does not steer us toward good thinking (remember the Paralysis Circle?). It does not steer us toward thinking at all. Winston Churchill once said, "Fatigue makes cowards of us all."

Exhaustion steers us toward mindless activities such as watching television. And guess what messages are waiting for us there?

So time is in short supply. But we need it to be on our side if we want to end up at our desired goal. The reality is that it takes very little time to begin to become a Shrewd Christian.

There are 10,080 minutes in a week. We only need 80 of those minutes to learn how to pay attention. I call them the Magic 80. Using those 80 minutes gives you the other 10,000 minutes to get on with your life. If you are married and each person takes on an 80-minute weekly financial focus, you really have the Magic 160. The Magic 160 amounts to 2.67 hours per week. You can do a lot in that amount of time. One spouse can form a preliminary plan; the other can figure out actual costs and waste. Then the two of you can review the other's research to figure out the best plan of action. All in 80 minutes.

It does not matter if you spend *more* than 80 minutes a week, but you must spend at least 80 minutes a week to make this plan work. You cannot spend less than 80 minutes each and every week.

Most people do not put time or thought into their financial plan. Therefore, they are reactive and dependent—reactive to events and dependent on others for solutions. The Magic 80 helps you think about finances and become proactive and independent—proactive by taking time to gain understanding, and independent by coming up with your own plan. Eighty minutes a week translates into over 69 hours a year. That is a little short of 2 weeks of *full-time work*. And, once again, if you are married and if your partner also does the Magic 80, WHOA! That would give you almost a month! You could answer any question if you had a month to work on it! Cool.

The idea is to use the Magic 80 to become Financially Alert. First of all, when you are in the middle of the Magic 80, you will discover that you are *not* shopping. That in itself will keep you out of trouble.

The first thing you should do when practicing the Magic 80 is pray. Two words are all that is necessary: "Lord, help!" If they were good enough for Peter as he was going down in a storm at sea, they are good enough for us as we are going through an economic storm. Prayer invites the Lord to take action. Now we have an Ally in this battle.

We have a spiritual Enemy. We live in a nasty culture. We are also our own enemy. (Remember the Gang of Three in chapter 3.) Let's see, if the math is correct, we are in deep weeds. Three to one. When you pray, the new math reads: Three to one and ONE. No contest, we win. (For a really humorous account of God as an ally, read 2 Kings 6.)

If you are married, report once a week on the thoughts and findings from your own Magic 80. This will get easier if you go on dates regularly. As you talk, make sure both parties feel heard. Sometimes it takes several meetings to make sure that each person is really heard.

The Magic 80 is the way to freedom. Let me say it again: You *must* spend at least 80 minutes a week working on your financial plan. You may spend more time, but you cannot spend less.

DISCOVERING HOW YOU SPEND MONEY

By now you have probably noticed something. We have not used the *b* word. We can say the word *budget,* but we will not put that word into practice. We do not need to. The two words that do not resonate with most of the American Middle Class are *diet* and *budgets*. That is because they do not work for most of America. Budgets and diets always encounter exceptions. They work for CPAs, business owners, and most engineers, but these people are not normal CMCers.

Take dieting for example. At first it sounds simple. Then one thing comes up that causes an exception. In my case, that one thing comes up once or twice every day. Research on dieting has shown that the majority of people who lose weight by dieting will not only gain that weight back, but they will put on additional pounds!

Budgets are like that as well; they usually do not last for the same reason. At first I liked budgets. Everything was spelled out for me: Housing should not exceed 35 percent of net spendable income; food should comprise no more than 13 percent, transportation no more than 18.5 percent, and so on. I had my little notebook and diligently entered the expenses under each listing. But I never could get the percentages to come out as they should. When I overspent the budget, I felt like a failure. When I underspent in one area, I would use that "extra money" in another area. After eighteen months, with some guilt, I stopped the budgeting process.

Did you ever get discouraged because you put together a budget that seemed very moderate, only to discover there was not enough income to cover your expenses? You looked and looked at where you could cut and, after frantic rearranging, you made the budget work. But it was bare bones and no margin (there's that word again) for error.

Single Tracking

So first, throw your budget away. You would have done it eventually anyway, so why not just get that task out of the way? Save yourself some trouble and guilt. Budgets are for nonnormal people. Budgets work for those people.

Second, you need accurate information that is customized to your real life. Remember the old Western movies? The bad guys were getting away, but some shrewd veteran said something like, "Looky here, by the one millimeter indentation in this set of tracks, we can see that they doubled up on their horses and sent the others out to mislead us. We figured it out and now we are on to them. Let's go."

You are going to become a shrewd veteran and track every cent of your expenses for forty days. Why forty days? Because forty is such a biblical number. Just as it took Moses forty years to get his people out of the wilderness, it will take you forty days to begin to get out of the financial wilderness. Therefore, begin to account for every penny you spend for the next six weeks. Every penny. Six weeks. Every person in the house. Every time you buy something, write it down. No exceptions.

Every seven days, total all of your expenditures (this is part of your Magic 80 for the week). After a little while you will see how you are spending your money, and you will notice that your expenditures fall into certain categories. Take note. This is called *tracking*. It is not new. I didn't invent it. (I first read about it in Mark Skousen's books.)

In *Your Money or Your Life*, Joe Dominguez and Vicki Robin add a helpful bit of advice to this exercise. To assure that there is no cheating and that each and every dollar is counted, they use the phrase "no shame, no blame."[1] There is no shame in giving accurate information. There is no blame attached to any expenditure, no matter how "silly" it appears.

At the end of six weeks, you will have a great amount of financial data. The hard part is now at hand. What is the hard part? You cannot list any expenses under "Miscellaneous." None. My accountant won't let me do it. I am not going to let you do it. The *m* word is a terrible killer of finances. Create new categories, but nothing goes under "Miscellaneous."

The secret to wealth is what you do *not* spend. Your tracking will not only tell you how you are spending your money but will acquaint you with opportunities to cut back on expenditures. As you track your money, wasted money will jump up and down to be noticed. It wants to be saved;

save it. But add it to assets, not lifestyle. Also, tracking expenditures will help you determine the value you received for your money. Little or no value? Why waste money on a similar expense in the future?

Double Tracking

If you are in debt, I suggest you do financial *double tracking.* This is a little more complicated, but still no shame, no blame. In addition to accounting for every penny spent, begin to write down every penny *not* spent. Here are some examples: You found a parking spot two blocks from the store and didn't feed the meter a dollar; you rented a movie for 99¢ at the grocery store instead of for $3.99 at the video store down the street. You didn't spend $4.

The purpose of single tracking is to let you know how you spend money and to develop a greater awareness of the real amount of money you spend. The purpose of double tracking is to make you aware of the amount of money you have in hand by not spending. In other words, you could have bought or spent, but you did not.

Margie's favorite breakfast restaurant is Marigold Café and Bakery. She spends $4 every morning. She wouldn't spend 40¢ if she ate breakfast at home, but I am *happy* that she spends the money. It is her way to start the day in a relaxed frame of mind. It would be stupid of me to say, "Let's cut out what is nurturing to you." We get value from Margie's Marigold experiences.

If Margie and I were in debt and the Marigold item showed up on our tally, we would talk about it. We would probably agree that she might visit Marigold only two times per week until we were on track. And we would agree to Margie's Marigold Reduction as long as I gave up something of equal importance to me. What would Neil's Equalizing Reduction be? I don't know, but it would be Win/Win or No Deal. We would then keep track of every morning Margie *didn't* spend that $4, and every day I didn't spend whatever I was giving up.

Making Your Savings Count

The purpose of double tracking is not only to give you an accurate idea of how you spend but to show you how easy it is to become generous, get out of debt, and accumulate financial wealth.

The double-tracking method allows you to make a game out of becoming generous and wealthy. And this game is for real. It will not only be fun but very productive. Figure out how you are spending your money and how your spending brings life and death. Then figure out how you're *not* spending your money—and invest in generosity or debt reduction.

So you have money coming at you in two ways: from cutting silly expenses and from finding opportunities to not spend money. If you merely take the savings and apply them to your lifestyle, you haven't saved a thing. Not shrewd. Take the amount you cut and add it to what you didn't spend. Write a check. Be generous. Pay down debt, or add to your accumulation fund. Shrewd.

THE VICTORY LIST

Here's another strategy for paying attention. No more surprises. Take a piece of paper or a marker board. List each month of the year at the top, from left to right. Enter each credit-card debt and its due date under your current month, and continue to enter the debt and the amount until it is paid off. Never again pay $29 a month. What happens when you pay off your credit-card debt? Write "vacation" in its place and take a good one in six months. Paid for in cash, of course.

Enter each family birthday under the appropriate month. (Family is anyone for whom you buy a gift or send a card.) Do the same thing for anniversaries, graduations, Valentine's Day, Mother's Day, Father's Day, Grandparents' Day. Write under the appropriate month when each insurance payment is due for life, home, auto, renter's, disability, long-term care. Include interest.

Enter your home taxes under the month they are due. (Feeling smug because your house insurance and taxes are part of your house payment? Enjoy and remember that feeling when you realize that by escrowing taxes and insurance, you are essentially renting your home. You are paying very little in equity. Your stomach will sink to the bottom of your heels. Bad place for a stomach to be.)

Enter seasonal clothes and school-supply purchases under the appropriate months. Enter the deductible you must pay for your yearly health needs: medical exam, dental, vision. Enter spring and fall auto maintenance. (Click and Clack, the *Car Talk* guys, say that the person who spends the least on regular auto maintenance will spend the most of all auto owners in the end.)

Enter April 15 under April. Enough said. Starting in August, enter "Christmas" under each month.

This is called your Victory List. Look at it every week as part of your Magic 80. You will see when the annual and semiannual bills are coming due. You will no longer be surprised, and you will start saving for them. It is natural. It is a lock. You are firmly on the road.

As you work with your tracking system and your Victory List, you will start to see the leaks in your financial plan. This doesn't necessarily mean you should stop spending money on those things. It *does* mean that you need to be aware of how much money you are spending in these areas and look for ways you might be able turn off any extra drips. And remember, you must always participate in the three nonnegotiables: generosity, taxes, and accumulation.

As you go, you'll find leaks or potential leaks that are unique to your own household. Don't mess around with them. Recognize them, write them down, and keep track of how much they are costing you. Figuring out how to stop them one leak at a time might be more fun than you think. And paying off debt, well, that's ecstatic fun any way you look at it.

COMPETITION CAN WORK FOR US

The Tough Shrewd Christian (TSC) loves competition in the marketplace because a TSC will actually force the market to compete. But (you guessed it) using comparison to force the marketplace to compete also means paying attention.

Let me illustrate: We were planning a trip to see our granddaughter, Riley, and, of course, Matt, Kellie, and Jodi. I checked my auto records. The coolant, transmission, and brake fluids were due to be changed in January, but since it was the middle of December and the trip was imminent, now was the time. Radiators and transmissions are necessary for traversing I-70 with a smile.

Enter competition. I called my new auto experts, Duh, Inc. Total price: $146.90. I called my old auto experts, Oops, Inc. Total price: $198.95. I called A2. He didn't want to discuss price on "piecemeal" business. He only sold services. Well, la-di-da! Scratch A2 from the Palm Pilot and let other import owners know to beware of him. A national franchise is only a few blocks from my office. Because they were a national outfit and could negotiate great deals, their prices would probably be best. The national outfit's price: $239.95.

So I saved $52.05 subtracting the best price from the second best, or $93.05 subtracting the best price from the worst. By forcing competition to reveal their true costs, we saved close to $100. Total time on phone: twenty-two minutes. Total hourly wage: $253. Do the math.

Let me give you another illustration in the art of alertness. I was happily minding my own business recently, and wouldn't you know it, the mail produced an inordinate amount of bills that day. I knew they were coming. I have the Victory List for a reason. But I didn't know the exact day of their arrival. It was today. Rather than switch to unhappily minding my own business, I gleefully played the game. I was prepared. And I was in the mood to do some damage to the bill senders. Today's mail had my semiannual insurance payment in it. Insurance people count on the fact that very few people practice the Magic 80.

I spent ninety minutes on the phone (okay, it wasn't eighty, but I was on a roll). I had my auto insurance papers with all the numbers in front of me. I called a few new insurance companies, got some information, and compared their rates with the rates of my current carrier. Results? I saved $441 by going with a new company. Not bad for an hour and a half. Shrewd.

The next month I received my house insurance bill. I noticed it had gone up 21.5 percent. I phoned four other companies. Pay dirt on the fourth call! I saved another $251 by switching carriers. Not bad for less than an hour's work. Total savings: $692.

Notice the difference between the above savings (you gain money by *not* spending it) and the "savings" of sales (you lose money by spending it on supposedly reduced-price goods).

Wait, it gets better.

One day I did a home energy audit. (Pulled it off our utility company's Web site.) Very helpful. Discovered lots of leaks. Plugged most of them. Saved $11 per month on the electric bill, $22 on gas, and $9 on water. Shoot, Neil, that is only $42. Big deal.

Next I hung up my cell phone: saved $45 per month. (Did you know that if you have a cell phone for emergencies, you don't have to pay for it? Just charge the batteries and carry the phone with you. If you are in an emergency situation, dial 911. The call is free.)

I then saw that the fax line was not critical. Saved $26. Eliminated my underground reserved parking spot at the office: $55.

Total savings from paying attention: $168 per month or $2,016 per year times thirty years, which is $60,480 (not including interest made on the money). To celebrate, I took Margie to Charles Court at the Broadmoor Hotel for her birthday. Spent a lot of money. She smiled a lot. Good value. Shrewd.

"Aha!" you say. "I just noticed that the last thing you did was very fun—and pleased Margie. The first things didn't impress me much. But the last thing—making your spouse happy—that impressed me. Hence, a clue. The first five actions were connected to saving, and the sixth action was properly connected to value spending."

You should be a sleuth. You could thwart crime. Save on Everything. Get Value for Everything. Do it every day and every week. Do it for a long period of time.

But hark! You want proof that I am not sending you on a wild goose chase. Okay, do it for a week. Add the savings for one week. Multiply by 52. Multiply by 30.

A locked and guarded back door (minimal out-go) provides the surest way to accumulation and wealth. But if you are not truly rich, a great defense can only result in financial wealth, and we must be truly rich as well as financially wealthy.

Financial Confidence comes from Financial Competence. Financial Confidence comes from Good Experience. Good Experience comes from accurate information.

If you *don't* pay attention, inaccurate information will fuel the leaks in your checkbook. Those leaks will accelerate at a faster pace than the income entering your checkbook. You will lose. If you *do* pay attention, accurate information will reduce and eventually stop the leaks in your checkbook. The newly plugged leaks will accelerate income entering your checkbook. You will win.

In the personal financial game, winning is everything. To repeat a critical question: What do you do with your "winnings"? (Read: the amount left over from the Save on Everything program.)

If you are like most people, your savings never really count for savings. Most people add any savings to their "lifestyle" spending. Most people are not shrewd. The spending-your-savings-on-your-lifestyle program continues to make us SLOBS (Slave Laborers of Bad Shepherds).

Shrewd means that you will record the savings in your checkbook (in a special color such as green), subtract the savings from your checkbook balance, and at the time of balancing your checkbook, total your savings. At that time you will write a check for that amount and either pay the Lord, pay down your debts (D1 and D2), or add to your accumulation fund. Either way, you have moved to the correct (right) side of the Not Wealth/Net Wealth Scale. Conversely, you have moved away from the left side of the scale (Not Wealth). You are making progress! You are becoming more shrewd.

STEPS TOWARD SHREWD

- Shrewdness comes from paying attention.
- Spend 80 minutes a week on your finances to increase your wealth.
- Use single and double tracking to increase your awareness of how much you are spending and not spending.
- Develop a Victory List that will end surprises.
- Learn how to make the market compete with itself to increase your savings!
- Do not channel your "winnings" back into your lifestyle.

8

Living Generously

According to the culture, you should accumulate as much money as possible so that you can buy things. The pervasiveness of this thinking is constantly reinforced by the countless messages of the Bad Shepherds. The culture says more money and more things will make you happy. But after reading the last few chapters, you now realize that you will never have "enough." Regardless, you have internal restlessness. You do not feel complete; something is wrong. You must do something. The emptiness that stems from feeling incomplete leads to deprivation, and that feeling in its unspiritual form gives birth to demand. Your demand leads to a department store; specifically, the sweater department.

You find the perfect sweater. You wear it to the party. Three people comment on how nice the sweater is and how nice you look in it. Twenty-seven people are jealous that you can afford the sweater and that you look so good, which results in zero comments on your sweater and your looks. You are unaware that they are jealous. You doubt your decision that what you have on is the perfect sweater. You start looking for another sweater.

How many sweaters on your shelf have you not worn in the past twelve months? How many sweaters did you give away in the last year? And how many perfect sweaters will make you perfectly happy?

God has a better plan. It doesn't have anything to do with sweaters.

Too many of us in the Christian Middle Class only give lip service to God when it comes to finances. I have a friend who happens to be a minister. My friend said there are not many atheists in his denomination, but there are a lot of practicing deists. Deism, as you may recall, is the belief that God started it all, but then sits back and allows us to handle the rest. It is like winding up a big clock, sitting in the recliner, and watching the hand sweep around the clock until the final tick and gong.

Many of the CMC are in a financial deist boat. They believe God is only involved in spiritual issues and that they must handle their own finances. When it comes to finances, most CMCers believe God helps those who help themselves. We are on our own. (I think I can hear taps beginning to play in the background.) It is not shrewd to shortchange the Lord!

When normal CMCers discover that the Getting/Having Syndrome as an answer to life is a lie, they usually look away and mumble some appropriate trite-ism, "Yeah, well, I guess I'll just have to let go and let God" or "I know I can't out-give God." The CMC is enmeshed in automatic spiritual Pavlovian responses that have no real meaning.

But as you know, God *does* care about every part of our lives, including our finances. He cares about our money not for the sake of our money but because our financial attitudes and actions reflect us as well as our attitude toward God. And our financial attitudes and actions can also *change* us as well as our attitude toward God. The truth is, the most important part of our financial life is our generosity.

The Paradox of Giving

One well-known author wrote a book on generosity. Note his opening remarks:

> During the time that I have worked on this book, I have been
> fairly secretive about the nature of my effort. On the few occasions
> when I tried to explain my intentions, people—including some of
> my best friends—gave me blank stares or simply said, "Oh." Stares
> and ohs do not elevate an author's enthusiasm for his project.…

After all, how do you explain that you are working on a book for Christian people who want to make living generously a high-priority goal in life? Most books are not about giving, but getting—getting riches, or success, or health, or happiness, or simply getting more informed. Do you see the problem?[1]

Do we *see* the problem? Come on, we *is* the problem. Recent statistics show a significant decrease in the number of people who tithe a portion of their income to the church. This statement is all the more startling because the percentage of tithers was already very low.[2]

The first change we have to make in our finance game is to decide to become generous. Starting now. It is not about what you have or what you are going to get; it is about what you are going to give. Money is the least of our gifts, but it is a good place to start.

You may be looking at those words and saying, "Oh no, I didn't see Neil sneaking up on me. He is going to make me feel guilty about not tithing. He doesn't understand my financial situation. I cannot afford to give money away, let alone tithe. I am sorry, but what can I do?"

Here's how I would respond to that statement: *If you can't afford to give, let alone tithe, you can't afford to be truly rich or financially wealthy, and you won't enjoy life as God meant you to enjoy it. In other words, you can't afford to be fully alive.*

It might seem strange to begin a game plan for developing financial wealth by giving money away and using money to build relationships. But one of the paradoxes from God is that life is found not in the *getting* or *having,* but in *giving.*

The lie: Having and getting result in life.

The truth: It is giving that produces life, not the illusionary getting or having.

How is that for a counterrevolution to financial terrorism?

Hear this! *You cannot be truly rich and financially wealthy without being a generous person.* Generosity is the key to true riches and financial wealth. Profound financial wealth can come our way if we will become generous people.

We are not becoming generous if we give to get. That takes us back to the lie. Giving to get is the antithesis of generosity. That is the error of the Prosperity Gospel. When we give, we should not look out of the corner of our eye for a flood of dollars to wash over us. Our reward is that we have entered God's economy. His economy is different from ours. We will not get a chance to review how our gifts were used until we are in touch with real reality in heaven.

But a volitional act of obedience—performing an act from our will and our head—will lead to emotional acts of obedience—performing from our heart. Jesus is not content with us as we are. He loves us as we are, but He loves us too much to let us stay as we are. He wants to change our hearts.

Most secular financial books say, "Pay yourself first!" That would not be generous; it would be selfish. And when you are selfish, you lose. The focus is me, me, me, and mine, mine, mine. That gets really old. So you buy things to feel better.

I say, "Pay the Lord first." If you give 10 percent of your gross salary, you are lessening your grip on yourself. That is, you are beginning to take the Lord more seriously and yourself less seriously. You are becoming more generous. You are living in faith.

Is it guaranteed that the Lord will reward you? Yes. Is it guaranteed that the Lord will reward you financially? No.

He *might* reward you financially—perhaps now, perhaps over time, or perhaps not at all. He is, after all, the Lord, and he isn't into making deals. He is into transforming us into generous, content, caring, loving, healthy people.

I can guarantee you one other outcome of being financially generous: If you give away 10 percent of your income, you will pay more attention to the remaining 90 percent. Paying attention means that you will not let impulsiveness cause you to throw dollars into the shredder. Paying attention means that you will Save on Everything and Get Value for Everything. Paying attention means that you will discover that you have more at the end of your giving. Before you know it, you will be living better on 90 percent than you did on 100 percent. Amazing how it comes together. And doesn't that play very nicely into the formula we learned earlier in the book?

So pay God first, and pay Him from your gross income. Early in our marriage, we argued about whether we should tithe from our gross or our net income. Fortunately, gross income won. What do you want the Lord to bless, the gross or the net?

The tax attorney for a recently deceased megabillionaire was asked, "How much did he leave?" He replied, "He left it all." If God owns it all, then we are responsible for what we do with what is His. Our possessions are really His possessions.

WARNING: If you do not agree with the previous paragraph, you had better run, not walk, to your Bible and reread (study) what Jesus said about money. Or would you rather take the word of the culture surrounding you?

If you are among the millions of Christians who cannot "afford" to tithe, then you are most likely living a lifestyle that shortchanges God, and that action will stop you from becoming truly rich (read: will impair your relationship with God) and financially wealthy. How did you get to the place where you cannot afford to tithe? One step at a time. How do you get back to this basic? One step at a time. Set a goal to tithe at least 10 percent within twelve months. But start by giving *something* now. Yes, it is work. But oh what a difference it will make in your life!

I know that some Christians fuss about the concept of tithing. The tithe is *law*. True Christians are under *grace*. Paying a tithe is undercutting the gospel. Yada-yada-yada. Nonsense. I like round numbers; 10 percent is easy to remember. And Jesus evidently liked round numbers too. He said to the Pharisees, "You give God a tenth of your mint, rue and all other kinds of garden herbs, but you neglect justice and the love of God. You should have practiced the latter without leaving the former undone" (Luke 11:42). If Jesus is for it, so am I.

The Law has no effect on Christians for initiating and maintaining a relationship with the Lord. The Law is not our master, Jesus is. However, the Law can serve as a guide or gauge to get us on the right track. If you want to give 10 percent, fine, do it—remember that God will probably ask you for more as you become wealthy. If you feel theologically queasy about the tithe, give 9.9 percent or 7.1 percent or 13.6 percent. But do it!

Richard Foster points out in *Money, Sex, and Power* that there are times when all of a family's tithe could and should be used for family difficulties.[3] I agree. He uses Mark 7:9-13 as the basis for this idea. He suggests that if our parents have a financial emergency, the correct thing to do is suspend the tithe for a time and give the money to our parents. Money is not our master; we are its master. Remember when Jesus took heat because His disciples were gathering grain on the Sabbath? His reply was classic: "The Sabbath was made for man, not man for the Sabbath" (Mark 2:27). Likewise, money was made for humankind; humankind was not made for money. We need to remember that—that is, if we want to be able to move on to true riches.

GUIDELINES FOR FINANCIAL GENEROSITY

Does God want us to be financially generous because He likes us to be uncomfortable, to let us know that He is in charge, that He needs the money? No, no, and big-time no. God loves us so much that He wants us to be generous primarily for what it will do for us! The purpose of money is to build relationships. When we give to Him, we are strengthening and building our relationship with Him. In other words, the generous giving of money can be a spiritual transaction.

It really is a heart thing. Do you give money to the Lord with an eye on the Lord? Good heart. Do you give money to the Lord with an eye on yourself (e.g., your name goes on the financial "honor roll," or on a building)? Fleshly heart. Do you give because you expect a reward? (That was a trick question to make sure you were paying attention. You did say no, didn't you?)

Giving a lot of money does not make a person generous. Giving a little money does not make a person generous. Giving no money most certainly does not make a person generous. Generosity begins and ends with the word *appropriate:* Appropriate generosity extended appropriately.

How we give is important. We are to give humbly: "Would you like your receipt with or without trumpets?" *Why* we give is important. We should give to the best of our ability: "Okay, Mr. Development Officer, I will count out $1,000 bills. Stop me as soon as I pass the gift of Harry and Maude." *How much* we give is important. Is our generosity determined by the organization or the Lord?

Here are questions we must all ask ourselves and answer honestly before God (simply asking them is not enough): (1) on what basis do we give money? (2) how much money do we give? and (3) how do we proportion it?

Would you believe that the vast majority of the "moneyed" are in the CMC? You are shocked: "Neil, you nitwit, the middle class is not 'moneyed'; it is the *middle* class." Yes, it is the middle class of the United States, but what about the world? There are approximately 6 billion people on the earth. Are you really going to tell me that 90 percent of the world wouldn't change places with us right now? Whether we own a home, rent an apartment, or live with our parents, 90 percent of the world would jump at the chance. To have security, shelter, clean water, indoor plumbing, a bedroom, and the right to voice an opinion is simply beyond the comprehension of the rest of the world.

"So are we to sell all, keep nothing, and give it all away?" People ask that defensive question because they feel they need to go on the offense, destroy my questions, and live happily ever after. Perhaps a good reply would be, "So are we to keep all, sell nothing, and give nothing away— or even more dangerous, dole out a politically correct amount here and there?" I doubt that we need to sell all. I do not doubt that all of us could become much more generous.

LEARNING TO GIVE

While we are working on true riches, we can work on financial wealth. Generosity is the beginning of the paved freeway to both true riches and financial wealth. Begin to give today. And if you are already a generous giver, ask the Lord if you could or should do more.

If He says, "Yes, you could and should give more," you may respond by asking, "Where will I find the money to do that?"

Perhaps you should give from principal, not earnings. (The sound you just heard was that of the beautiful people fainting.) Perhaps the Lord is suggesting you expand your business and use the additional profit to give. In a recent conversation, a friend mentioned a person who lives on 10 percent of his earnings and gives 90 percent away.

Perhaps you should ask for a raise. Perhaps God is getting frustrated that you have stayed in the wrong job for too long.

Perhaps, even more simply, He expects you to find a financial drip, fix it, and give the money away.

You can start by giving money to your church, if you feel that the Lord is leading you to do this. You will know He is leading you to do this if you are currently giving nothing or very little to your church. Your church will thank you.

Do you know someone in a ministry who is doing a good job? Call him or her up and ask if you could help with a financial contribution. Do you know how unbelievably encouraging it will be to that person?

Do you have a rescue mission in your city that feeds, clothes, and provides shelter for the poor? Send money. You will get on a bunch of mailing lists, but it is the right thing to do ("Whatever you did for one of the least of these…" [Matthew 25:40]).

Okay, you are becoming generous. What will happen as a result of your giving? Well, we will never have the complete picture of how the Lord used our generosity until we enter the gates of heaven. Everything will then be exposed for what it was, even the motivations behind our gifts.

In the meantime I can promise you this: Generosity will help you focus on truth, and that will lead you to handle the rest of your income in a wise manner. However, the main effect is that your insides will begin to work in a new way: You will have more internal godly confidence. You will find that your generosity will expand into other areas of your life…for all the right reasons.

Steps Toward Shrewd

- God cares about your finances.
- Generosity is one way to become truly rich. You may also become financially wealthy in the process.
- God wants to transform us into generous and content people.
- God owns it all.
- *How, why,* and *how much* you give is important.

9

Dealing with Debt

P rofit is the business god of the United States. Profit is how business-people keep score. Oversimplified, profit is the difference between the selling price of an item and the cost involved in getting that item produced and sold. (Remember that salaries are part of cost. Profit is on top of that.) The more costs can be lowered and the higher the selling price can be pushed, the better the profit. Competition among providers is what is supposed to keep prices from going through the roof.

Since the Shrewd Christian is at war with those who make profit from our expenditures, we should thwart them: Let's minimize their profit. That means they will make less money. But it also means we will have more money. In other words, we will profit from their lack of profit. We accomplish that by finding more life for less money!

A major profit center for most corporations is debt (sticking debt on you and me). You may know the words of the song "Sixteen Tons":

You load sixteen tons, what do you get?
Another day older and deeper in debt...
I owe my soul to the company store.[1]

The company store used to be a grim reminder of unrestrained greed. Workers received a wage for their efforts, but due to the location of their employment and their lack of mobility, they had to rent housing from their employers. In addition, the company owned the only available store. Not pretty.

Today the company store is better known as our credit system. If you owe money, you are owned. Your friendly banker pays you 0.75 percent on your checking account and lends that money to prospective home buyers at 6.5 percent. The spread between what the bank pays you for the money and what it loans out is the profit. Okay, okay, they have overhead. Somebody has to pay for the starched white shirts and suspenders. But the drift is in the right direction.

The people who lend you money are the real owners of everything you have in your possession. When push comes to shove, the law supports the lender, not the borrower. They ain't your friends. They may smile. They may call you "Mr." or "Ms.," but they ain't your friends. They are after profit, not relationship. If they can have both, fine; if not, they will take profit. They are predators who want to tear you to pieces by owning you. The ones I hate the most are the Christian wolves dressed as sheep.

All right, time for an economics test. I think everyone will get an A. If the bank can have the choice between loaning a person money at (a) 6 percent, or (b) 18 percent, which would give the bank more profit?

I knew you were good. Right answer. Way to go.

Thus credit cards were born. They are much more profitable than home loans.

As early as the 1950s, credit cards were just getting started. Until then, people did an astounding thing: They saved money for things and bought those things with cash. Buying on credit was frowned upon by most people.

But then credit became easy. At first you had to be "special" to get a credit card. That created envy in the nonspecial people; envy created demand and demand created credit cards for nonspecial people. America's middle class had arrived; they could have it all. Now. They did not have to wait thirty years for luxuries; their credit could help them immediately "afford" the things that had taken their parents decades to acquire.

But somehow easy credit backfired on the American public; debt levels, foreclosures, and stress skyrocketed. Fortunately, there were alternatives if credit cards dried up.... For example, pawn shops have been around a long time. For those of you who frequent pawn shops for the purpose of procuring money rather than goods, your interest rate is around 70 percent. And for those of you who frequent payday loan places, your interest rate is around 700 percent.

The Old Testament had a word for all this: *usury*. At one time, federal and state usury laws in the United States limited amount of interest banks could charge. But a 1978 Supreme Court decision deregulated banks, making it possible for them to charge interest without limits as long as they operate out of states that no longer have usury laws. This means banks have the legal right to enslave you, skin you, and tack your hide to the side of their buildings. If you let them, they will own you. Don't let them. Don't let mortgage companies own you. Don't let automobile finance companies own you.

Own yourself. You will be in much better shape to walk with the Lord. It was the Lord, if memory serves me correctly, who paid a high price for you. Don't sell a part of yourself and your family to a banker.

All of us must, at all costs, avoid becoming SLOBS (Slave Laborers of Bad Shepherds). If we are in debt, we are slaves. We *have* to keep working to pay off the stuff. If our kids get sick or we want an education or our parents need us or we want to hit the Bahamas for a year or two, tough, we are SLOBS. God is calling us to serve Him in another part of the world? *I am sorry, Lord, you know I would like to, and I am sure you understand. I will be free some day. But right now, the answer is no, Lord.* ("No, Lord" is, by the way, an oxymoron.)

I had my annual visit with my accountant recently. It is a tossup as to whether I would rather visit my accountant or my dentist. The dentist hurts a little bit, but I feel numb not dumb when I leave his office. However, anyone who can do battle with our tax code concerning corporations or businesses is either a very smart person or a masochist. I need a smart person.

Anyway, I told Marc about this book and that one of its basic premises is living completely free of debt. It did not surprise me that he was surprised by my statement. He raised his eyebrows (as only CPAs can do) and said, "*All* debt?"

"Yep." I then plunged ahead and said, "Tell me something good about debt."

He looked a little bewildered and said, "Most people need it to get into their first house."

I said, "I agree, but they don't need thirty-year mortgages."

Marc then talked about individuals who used OPM (Other People's Money), acquired a piece of land, and in a few years made an impressive gain.

"Marc, this book is for the Christian Middle Class. Let me tell you why the CMC are not millionaires. We don't like risk. It is a good thing we don't like risk. I agree that there are individuals who have a talent for forecasting financial trends and get themselves in front of those trends. But that is why millionaires are a minority in this country. Nine out of ten new businesses fail in the first five years. Over 20 percent of *personal* bankruptcies are caused by business failures. The odds do not favor the middle-income person."

Marc: "Aren't you forgetting inflation?"

"Nope. While it's true that medical costs have gone up 223 percent since 1980, it is just as true that the cost of a gallon of gas today is the same as it was thirty years ago. And the price of chicken is less than it was thirty years ago. The consumer price index (CPI) is for economists and financial people. The CMC will not buy a new house every week, nor a car, nor a refrigerator. Personal inflation will be less, much less, than the experts would have us believe."

Marc and I ended on a good note. He was jovial if not convinced. That's what $175 per hour will do for you.

What I am saying here, in case it's been a bit vague, is that I am against debt! We are going to beat lenders at their own game. It *is* shrewd to short-change the people who are out to own us. Not by cheating, but by getting rid of debt. But first we have to know what kind of debt we are dealing with.

The Three Ds

There are three kinds of debt: devastating, decent, and delightful. The first two are those you want to eliminate from your life; the third is the one you want in your life.

1. Devastating Debt is the debt we pay for *depreciating* items. If we took a very nice vacation to Disney World in February but are still paying for it in August of the same year, we have in front of us a perfect example of Devastating Debt. "But we were all exhausted from our work, and we *needed* that time away." At 19 percent, I might add.

Another example: "We needed a new car. The old one was dirty and there was actually dust on the interior!" Some of you are smiling. You just bought a car but didn't pay *any* interest. No, you didn't. But you do owe a lot money for a piece of machinery that lost 20 percent of its value the moment you drove it off the lot. And you are paying the tax, registration, and insurance based on the new-car price.

2. Decent Debt is the debt we pay for *appreciating* items. For example, most homes in most parts of the country advance in price every year. (Unless, of course, you are in a more depressed area, your neighborhood has gone downhill, or you found out your home was built over a toxic landfill.) Antique furniture is the only furniture that has a possibility of rising in value.

3. Delightful Debt is the debt (dividends and interest) that others (companies, businesses, banks, the government) owe you.

Margie and I flirted with debt-free living when we lived in Michigan and achieved it in Kansas and Colorado. The hardest financial lesson I learned is that I could not compete as an amateur with men and women who make their livings as professionals. That is true whether it is real estate, autos, clothes, insurance, or groceries. The professional has more in his or her bag of tricks than I could possibly counter. Until I became shrewd. And you can be too.

WHY CREDIT-CARD DEBT IS NOT TOTALLY YOUR FAULT

Think of the uproar there would be if the names of recovering alcoholics, pornographers, child abusers, and gamblers were sold to businesses that produced that garbage. Then if the marketing departments of these businesses sent out weekly solicitations in the mail: "Free drinks!" "Pretty pictures!" "Children's catalogs!" "Hot tips guaranteed to win!"

We wouldn't say, "Well, too bad. You don't have to open the letters. It is your fault." We would be sympathetic and outraged. We would be angry. These offers would be putting obstacles in the paths of people trying to create a new life. Something would have to be done!

As far as I know, these kinds of disasters are not happening, but something similar is happening in another area. Every week creditholics receive more credit-card offers in the mail. People already overextended get tempting "introductory" offers that will "help" them. People who pay the minimum balance are the lawful prey of banks.

And we are not outraged, nor are we demanding that something be done. Instead, we are heaping guilt on people by saying, "Well, too bad. You don't have to open the letters. It is your fault."

Get a grip. The offers of "help" are merely greed in its most poisonous form: socially accepted greed that puts the blame on the victim. The credit industry wants people to think that being ensnared by too much debt is totally the responsibility of the individual. Article after article in money magazines tsk-tsk over "undisciplined" spenders. Those spenders are forced to admit their financial sins in front of the nation, and then "experts" give advice to the miscreants.

Please notice that you seldom (if ever) see articles chastising the financial industry for aggressiveness in issuing irresponsible credit. ("Why do you suppose that is true, Neil?" "Why, friend, money magazines will not bite the hand that feeds them. Do you see why the credit industry must bear some responsibility for your credit-card debt?")

If you are late with a payment, if your credit rating takes another hit, or if the credit-card company simply wants to do so, the interest rates can increase. And what happens when the "low introductory rate" runs out? Yes, you are still responsible for the total amount you owe. No, it is not all your fault. And no, the other party who caused you to go into debt will *not* help you out of your debt. *Their profit depends on your debt.*

Credit-card debt is different from any other debt in four ways:

1. The loan issuers come to you through mail solicitations—constant mail solicitations.
2. The confirmation process requires only that you are breathing—anybody can get credit.
3. Instead of having a fixed amount of money to pay off (such as a home loan), you are paying on an expanding loan amount.
4. The interest rate is huge. Pay attention to that last statement. You are profit. You are fresh meat to the credit carnivores.[2]

Credit-card debt in the United States is averaged two different ways. If you are a member of the credit-card industry, you will say that the average American has $8,000 in credit-card debt. That is true. But not totally true.

Robert Manning reports that 43 percent of Americans are using credit cards correctly. They are paying the balance each and every month. (I find it interesting that the number of such people was only 29 percent as recently as 1996. People just might be catching on to the game.) Manning calls such people "convenience users." The credit-card industry calls them "deadbeats." (My, my, haven't times changed? Used to be that people who *didn't* pay bills were described that way.)

This means that 57 percent of credit-card users are revolvers (they do not pay the balance every month). If we look at the revolving-debt segment as the only group that actually has credit-card debt, then the amount owed by Americans is much higher than the United States average invented by the marketing department of the credit-card lobby. An amazing 37 percent higher! The average American who pays interest on his or her credit-card loan is well over $11,000 in credit-card debt![3]

Credit-card debt is nondeductible interest—you may not include it as an interest deduction on your tax form. You are getting drilled. And your owner keeps raising your credit-card limits because you are such a good customer! Who is winning this war?

If you are deeply in debt, the first thing to do to get out of debt is to stop using your credit cards. Now. Cut up every one except one—the one with the lowest interest rate and no annual fee. Put that card in the freezer in a Ziploc bag filled with water. Do not touch it until you are out of Devastating Debt. Or unless you experience a true emergency, such as a health crisis.

After you are out of Devastating Debt and securely on the road to true riches and financial wealth, you can use credit cards to your advantage and beat the BSers. For example, you can use your credit cards to accumulate airplane mileage. Mileage means money. I get one mile for every dollar I spend using my credit card.

Recently, my wife threw a 75th birthday party for her dad. The party was held in Seattle. Our family was spread around the country—Colorado Springs; Overland Park, Kansas; and Waco, Texas. To get everyone there on a timetable that wouldn't interfere with work was going to cost a lot.

However, I had bunches of banked miles because of travel and credit-card purchases (which were always paid in full on time and therefore did not cost one cent of interest). I used those miles and saved over $2,500.

(How much would we have had to earn to net $2,500?) Oh, yes, I paid a $60 fee for the use of the card.

I think I won this round, don't you?

INTEREST IS A SPENDING CATEGORY

What spending category takes the most amount of your income? You immediately reply, "Housing." You are wrong. By a wide margin. Even if you add in utilities, insurance, and maintenance, housing is light years away from your largest spending category. That category is called "Interest." Realizing that fact alone will help you to move toward the goal of Financial Alertness.

Grab a piece of paper. Across the top write:

Tithe   *Taxes*   *Savings*   *Interest (Rent)*

We need to put that information in front of us.

What is going on here? (Remember, *interest that you pay is nothing more than rent due on the money you took from someone.*) Let's say that you have just completed your first year of house payments, car payments, and credit-card payments. How much interest did you pay every month?

- Interest on the house: You borrowed $100,000 at 7 percent over thirty years; therefore, your monthly payment is $665. For twelve months you average $85 for principal and $580 for interest.
- Interest on the car(s): You borrowed $20,000 at 6.75 percent over 5 years; therefore, your monthly payment is $394. For twelve months you average $290 for principal and $104 for interest.
- Interest on bank credit cards: Let's see…you are an average American with revolving credit-card debt of $11,000. Let's assume that sometimes you make inroads on the balance and sometimes you have to skip a payment. (We will postpone worrying about annual fees, late payment fees, and hikes in interest rates as a result of late

payments.) You are financing your lifestyle at $11,000 at 17.5 percent over ten years; therefore, your payment is $194. For twelve months you average $37 for principal and $157 for interest.

- And interest on department store and gasoline credit cards? Even your doctor has easy payment plans. We really would feel better if we did not include these items. Of course, that would be delusional.

Total monthly interest payments of the first three bullets: $837, or $10,044 per year, or *$27 per day.*

What? You are correct. I did not take taxes into account. But remember, only house interest is deductible. $576 x 12 = $6,912 x 25% = $1,728 in a tax deduction! Whoopee! You still had to pay $5,184 in interest.

We redo the math, and it comes to a total of $8,316 per year, $693 per month and *$23 per day.* How much of what you make is going to interest? Oops.

Interest is so powerful that it's worth looking at more closely....

Compound Interest

Albert Einstein was once asked, "What is the greatest mathematical phenomenon on earth?" His reply? "Compound interest!" This from one of the greatest minds the world has ever seen. Half of the readers are thinking, "Duh, everyone knows that!" and the other half are thinking, "Huh?" But the latter are too embarrassed to say anything.

The following is for all of the embarrassed people. First, words. Then a diagram. Compound interest will work *for* or *against* you. This is economic gravity. And it leads you toward the *Finish* or the *Start* of the Not Wealth/Net Wealth Scale.

Let's look at the positive side first. Interest is what you earn on your savings. Compound interest begins when the interest that you earned on your savings makes more money just by itself. Then the new interest, plus past interest, makes more money by itself. You end up with this picture:

$$\$ + PI = I \text{ (year 1)}$$
$$\$ + PI + PI = I \text{ (year 2)}$$
$$\$ + PI + PI + PI = I \text{ (year 3)}$$
$$\$ + PI + PI + PI + PI = I \text{ (year 4)}$$

Etc. (years 5–30)

START	Picture Black Ink Here!	FINISH
Financial Claustrophobia		Financial Confidence
Lifestyle		Assets
NOT WEALTH		NET WEALTH

Notice that this pattern moves you closer to your goal—you are going in the right direction. You are heading to the right side of the scale, toward Net Wealth and Financial Confidence. And that is all there is to it. Compound interest will get us from Financial Claustrophobia to Financial Confidence. It is one of the reasons why there is no such thing as a "little amount of money."

Take a lowly one dollar bill. Instead of spending that dollar, let's accumulate and maintain it at 5 percent for thirty years. I know, I know. It is a small amount of money and your coworker knows a guy who can get you 18 percent—guaranteed! But humor me.

One dollar at 5 percent over thirty years will become $4.46. That is not a lot of money. (Don't leave now! There's more!) Now let's say that you decide to accumulate one dollar a day and protect those 365 dollars at 5 percent over thirty years. You will have $7,148. I see the light beginning to go on in your eyes. What would happen if you could save $10 per day and do it for thirty years?

But remember the little fact about compound interest being able to work *against* you? That's where debt rears its ugly head. Let's look at the diagram from another angle. This is what debt and compound interest look like over time:

$$(\text{year } 1)\; D = PD + \$$$
$$(\text{year } 2)\; D = PD + PD + \$$$
$$(\text{year } 3)\; D = PD + PD + PD + \$$$
$$(\text{year } 4)\; D = PD + PD + PD + PD + \$$$
$$(\text{years } 5\text{–}30)\; \text{Etc.}$$

START	Picture Red Ink Here!	FINISH
Financial Claustrophobia		Financial Confidence
Lifestyle		Assets
NOT WEALTH		NET WEALTH

If you rent one dollar, you must pay back that dollar plus the interest due on it. If you cannot afford to pay back that dollar and only pay a minimum amount, the second payment will include the dollar, plus previous interest, plus interest on the previous interest. The third payment will include the dollar you owe plus interest, previous interest plus interest on the previous interest, and so on.

Which direction are you heading? You are heading to the left side of the scale, to Not Wealth and Financial Claustrophobia. Notice that you are moving *away* from your goal. You are moving in the wrong direction! That route is not getting you where you want to go. It is getting greedy, rich guys where *they* want to go. If you are buying into the left side of that pyramid, you are making sure that *they* win and *you* lose. You owe them. Therefore they own you. Money has mastered you.

There is no such thing as a small amount of debt, just as there is no such thing as a small amount of calories. Did you know that if you take in just ten more calories than you expend in a day, you will gain a little more than a pound in one year? Times twenty-five years? It gets worse. Not only will you have gained fat, you will have lost muscle. The truth is that you will put on about thirty to thirty-five pounds of *fat*. The picture is not pretty.

Every dollar that goes to serve those who own a piece of you—the lenders—is one dollar that you do not have to invest in Financial Confidence and Financial Freedom. One dollar invested at 5 percent for thirty years will give you $4.46. One dollar that you give to your owner at 19 percent over thirty years will take $285.81 from you. What happens if you give $10 per day over thirty years to your owner?

Okay, let's up the ante; we are going to use $1,000 as our base. Most of us could get $1,000 tomorrow if we absolutely had to have the money. Many of us owe at least $1,000 on our credit cards. Saving $1,000 at 5 percent for thirty years is $4,467.74—a positive future value. Owing $1,000 at 19 percent for thirty years is $285,815—a *negative* future value.

Remember the Bad Shepherds? They want compound interest to work *against* you and *for* them. Now, I am a businessperson. I understand profit. It is good. Greed, however, is not good. Greedy players use the culture to develop competition and comparison within us to create insatiable desires. Even though you are not *in* debt due to only your efforts, you will get *out* of debt entirely by your own efforts. That means you have to pay attention, cultivate contentment, and resist the Bad Shepherds around you. It causes some pain at first, and then a little more pain, second. Third, you'll feel a blast of fresh air, and finally, the glorious reality of freedom.

Many financial experts say, "Build a savings cushion while you get out of debt. It is important to do both at the same time. Otherwise, in an emergency, you will have to use credit."

I say, "Devastating Debt is so bad, use every dollar just to get out of it. If an emergency happens, you still have that credit card. You have tasted freedom and you will not become a slave again!"

Remember the words of Jesus: "Come to me, all you who are weary and burdened.… Take my yoke upon you and learn from me.… For my yoke is easy and my burden is light" (Matthew 11:28-30).

STEPS TOWARD SHREWD

- The people who lend you money *own* you.
- Do you have Devastating Debt, Decent Debt, or Delightful Debt? Getting rid of Devastating Debt is the only way you will become wealthy.
- You are fresh meat to the carnivores who offer credit cards.
- Interest is a spending category.
- Use compound interest to help you move away from Financial Claustrophobia to Financial Confidence.

10

Becoming a Residential CEO

Thomas Stanley is an expert on millionaires. One of his findings, contrary to television and other media, is that the vast majority of earned millionaires are frugal people. Stanley has coined a phrase that is characteristic of most millionaire households. He states that millionaires have "economically productive households."[1] The EPH is central to the Christian Middle Class becoming Shrewd Christians and developing winning attitudes and strategic game plans.

Though Margie and I didn't use those words, we did find out early in our marriage that living frugally at home made a big difference in our finances. We were too busy doing ministry and having fun to realize that we were below the poverty line. But we were also, unwittingly, accumulating financial wealth. The secret was that one of us served as the Residential CEO. One of us was in charge of constantly paying attention to how we were spending and not spending money. For most of our marriage, Margie served in that capacity. For the past eight years, I have filled that role. Our roles have changed as our careers and places of residence have changed. But *one* of us has to be the RCEO of our home if we are going to maintain financial wealth.

I am hereby appointing you as the RCEO of your household. (The words housewife, househusband, and homemaker are hereby eliminated.) You are on commission only—what you don't spend, you get to keep. Your mission is to make sure you turn your home into an EPH: an Economically Productive Household.

Thirteen separate economic entities make up the home: Building and grounds, transportation, insurance, taxes, tithe, food service, cleaning, apparel, benefits, accounting, investing, research and development, and purchasing. If you own a home, you should see these thirteen segments as divisions. If you are a good RCEO of every division in your household corporation will become productive and will lead toward wealth. This is a full-time job. Do it well.

Job Description

You have to understand a few guidelines before you begin your job as an RCEO. This is a career, not a walk in the park. At first you will work harder than you ever have. But you will have a ball doing it. Soon you will realize that your efforts are crucial to developing Net Wealth. You will be slaying the profit dragon that has been terrifying your household.

If you're married, one spouse will be bringing home most of the income—that which comes in the front door. The other spouse should be protecting and maximizing the income—locking and guarding the back door. Income is precious and you must minimize spending. Minimizing costs is your goal!

Danger: If you are a full-time RCEO and do not have a job outside your home, some of your friends, neighbors, and relatives might see you as fair game to meet *their* needs.

"Bob, since you don't work for a living, would you mind looking after Angel after school? I would offer to pay you, of course, but I know you are not a greedy person."

"Glenda, I am absolutely done in by my two jobs, to say nothing of entertaining Harry's clients every weekend. I know you have a lot to do (I can't *imagine* how you spend your days and how boring it must be), but I need some help getting Mom to her eye doctor appointment. Would you be a dear and take her for me? I will reimburse you for transportation if you insist…"

You do not have time to become the doormat of the neighborhood. Put this picture in your mind: If you say yes to *their* families' needs, you are saying no to *your* family's needs. Your choice. After you are out of debt and on solid financial ground, you might be able to loosen up if that is your desire.

Again, an RCEO's purpose is cost containment. Alertness. Paying attention. This is what will bring wealth. Don't expect too much too soon. This is where another table manner comes into play: ingenuity. It will take you several days or weeks to begin to grasp the intricacies and significance of what you are doing. You will need to add your own enthusiasm and ingenuity to the recipe. Give yourself a month or two to get a handle on the game. Call it a conditioning program toward toughness.

As RCEO, you will keep a record of spending—how much money you rescued from the trash bin—and review it at the end of every week. Let the fun begin.

YOUR FIRST WEEK ON THE JOB

Welcome! As RCEO, you have ultimate responsibility for all the divisions of your corporation. Your primary job is to Save on Everything and Get Value for Everything.

Here is the formula that will overcome backward gravity or inertia:

$$LT + E(T) + A^2 = FC^{10}$$

Little Things done Excellently over Time and Applied Appropriately will result in Financial Contentment to the Tenth Power.

As the race announcer says, "People, start your engines!" Let's get to your first day on the job.

First, *set up an Information System.* Emblazon the name of each division in your home on a file folder. No, this is not a filing system; those are bland and boring. This is an Information System (IS) that will lead you to wealth. Make sure the IS is located in one place, not in a few folders in your desk and a few in the kitchen. Gather all of your records (bills, invoices, policies, receipts, warranties, etc.) and file them. Nothing may be labeled "Miscellaneous."

Next, *arrange a Research and Development System.* The first step to an effective Research and Development System is to cut out anything you read that is helpful to you (unless it is from a library book) and put in the proper file. This applies to notes you make on your adventures.

For example, we had a problem with morning and early afternoon sun on our deck. In Colorado, summer is short, and we want to maximize it by spending as much time as we can outside. The problems were strong sun, strong wind, and rain. We needed a deck cover that would take care of all those conditions. Yet it could not be a permanent structure because that would block our view of the bluff behind us.

So over the course of several months, when I read an article or saw an advertisement for an awning, I cut it out and put it in the "House" file. When we visited home shows, I picked up appropriate literature. The local expert wanted $1,900 for an awning that could not stay up in the wind and wasn't rainproof. I kept looking. Finally, my eyes caught sight of an awning that was retractable, wind-stable, rainproof, offered sun protection, and was endorsed by *Good Housekeeping!* Shoot, if it was good enough for Betty Crocker or Martha Stewart or whoever the latest guru was, it was fine by me. The price? $889, shipped. Keeping track of information helped me get the best deal with the least amount of hassle. As RCEO of this project, I solved the problem and saved $1,011.

By the way, you do know about *Consumer Reports,* don't you? If not, please meander down to your local library. Take out a lot of the back issues. *Consumer Reports* is our teammate in the game of Financial Confidence.

Next, do a *home audit* and figure out what assets you have to work with. Oh baby, if you only knew how much you had. Not knowing means you have a blind spot. Let's shine some light on that blind spot. You will take a real (as opposed to a virtual) tour of your house and inventory your assets. You will see your home differently if you just look at one part of one room.

Go to the kitchen. Time for a little organization. Stare at the refrigerator. The refrigerator is your friend. Are you taking care of this friend? How long have the pictures been on the front? Do you still like them? Keep them. Open the freezer door. Grab the corn before it hits the floor. Good job. Take everything out and put it on the counter. Carefully wipe out the crumbs. Remove the sticky residue that stops the door from closing completely. Wash the grime inside.

Review what is on the counter. Think: *How long have some frozen articles been living in the cold?* If a few of them have grown mold even in the freezer; they might enjoy a scenic trip to the dump. Put everything that is going the way of all flesh in a cardboard box. Do not make a trip to the garbage just yet. I know you are afraid that if some of this food thaws, it may come after you. Worry not.

You say you have three half-gallons of ice cream with beautiful ice crystals all over them? Do not throw them away! Rinse the crystals off under water. Combine the three into one. Make a milk shake for the kids when they come home from school. Shoot, you might as well make one for yourself.

What else? Leftovers that no one liked in the first place? You are expecting a miracle that somehow they will like them now? Toss. Now where did these five bread bags come from? Combine the five into one and make French toast for dinner. Yes, dinner. Are you aware that kids will eat breakfast for dinner and not know it is a poor-folks' meal? Your family will love it, and you are clearing space for this money-making machine.

Now that you know what in the freezer will work for you and what you can serve in the immediate future, plan meals to use that food. Do not shop for dinners until the freezer is depleted. Figure out how much you will save by (1) not spending current money for dinners, and (2) consuming what you bought before it spoils from lack of attention.

Not that much? Our credo is: A lot of Little Things done Excellently over Time and Applied Appropriately will bring wealth. True, it is a little thing. It may be your first little thing, but it will not be your last little thing.

Put the stuff that made the cut back in the freezer. Way to go! Take a thirty-second break. Step back. Stare at the refrigerator. There is one more door.

You know the drill. When the goods are on the counter and the refrigerator is clean, shut the door on a dollar bill. If you can pull the dollar out of the door, you may have to replace the gasket. A new refrigerator is hundreds of dollars; a new gasket is a few dollars. The friendly guy at Sears will tell you how to do this.

What can you lose immediately from your fridge? Hmm, the fungus is really camouflaging whether that is a sauce or a dressing. Rats, I didn't know the bacon was under different cheeses. Goodness, was that a cucumber or a zucchini? Throw all of them away. Combine what you can. One bottle of ketchup is more efficient than two bottles; one jar of pickles is better than two jars.

Restock the refrigerator. Try not to overload the door. Too much weight can throw the door out of whack and result in repairs or loss of efficiency.

Now what meals can you make with what you have in your refrigerator? List them. Action: You will not buy new dinner things until you have consumed current dinner things.

Bring pencil and paper to the wastebasket. As carefully, accurately, and honestly as you can, list the stuff that is going bye-bye and write down an estimate of wasted dollars. It has been said that American families waste 15 percent of their food. What is your tally? Wait, is that a chicken carcass in your waste box, along with a few damaged onions and carrots?

Rescue them. Put them in a pot with boiling water. Homemade chicken stock. You didn't waste it after all. Redo your tally. Way to go!

Your freezer and refrigerator will soon be full of *really* inexpensive and delicious food. You will be glad it has space to accommodate the good stuff.

Let's say you spend $135 a week on food (the average a family of four spent in 1998). If the above figure of 15 percent waste is accurate, you are throwing away $20 per week or $1,040 per year or $41,600 in your adult years. How much did you waste in the end? If yours is a normal family, the amount was probably a tidy sum of money. Remember the credo.

Look what you accomplished to this point: (1) you developed an IS system, (2), you developed your R&D System research, *and* (3) you reorganized a money-saving instrument. (Hint: If we eliminate most waste and discover additional strategies to lower the cost of groceries, we have a double play going! See chapter 12 for more details.)

Do the above exercise on your pantry, laundry room, medicine cabinets, and other storage spaces.

Next, we will work on eliminating financial surprises. At times our lives can seem to move at the speed of light. Often we get into a fast-moving life rhythm in which we forget about quarterly, semiannual, or annual bills.

It is the unanticipated or forgotten expenses that deflate most people. You are feeling okay about your finances—finally, a little breathing room. And then BAM! A bill for life insurance shows up on the same day as the department store credit-card bill. And wouldn't you know it, a filling in your tooth is loose and the maintenance light is showing bright orange in your automobile. So much for breathing room.

This is why you need your Victory List (see chapter 7). Part of your shrewd toughness is an every-week review of this chart. Glance at the present month and the next two months—you do not have to study it or meditate over it. Is anything heading your way for which you need to be prepared?

Now you're ready to focus on the specific divisions of your home corporation. Some of those divisions have whole chapters of their own, but we'll focus on a few here that particularly pertain to the everyday maintenance of your house.

BUILDING AND GROUNDS

Home maintenance is a *big* opportunity to save money and develop wealth. This is a major area in which we middle-income people differ from millionaires. Very few millionaires do their own lawn care and repairs. The CMC is not them—we is us, and we will service and repair most of our stuff. Because we are very coachable and tough, we will also learn to be ingenious. Do not be discouraged if you have difficulty telling the difference between a hammer and a paintbrush.

If you are not very handy, it will take you three to four times as long as a professional. Who cares? You are saving after-tax dollars (the most valuable kind), and you will gain experience and confidence. You will become "handier" than you were before you started the project. If you are not very handy *and* you are an intense or anxious person, be careful and give yourself more time and more grace to accomplish things.

On my daily run in Grand Rapids, Michigan, I noticed that someone had thrown a recently cut small evergreen tree into a vacant lot. It was November, and we needed a Christmas tree. This little tree was green, had a semblance of the shape of a Christmas tree, and it was free. Perfect. I rescued that tree from loneliness and decay and filled its last days with dignity and joy. (Poverty meets enthusiasm and ingenuity.)

Rescuing the tree was fun; making it work in our living room was not fun. Would I do that again? If we were in the same financial circumstances, I would do it in a heartbeat. A few years later I bought an artificial tree. On sale. Still using it.

I do enjoy lawncare and gardening. These are two productive hobbies that mean I am spending time and money improving the curb and entertainment appeal of our home. And I am not spending money losing golf balls.

When we have dinner guests, they arrive to a beautifully maintained and landscaped front yard and entrance to our home. In the summer they love to sit on our deck because the backyard is very inviting.

I designed my yard with aesthetics and pragmatics in mind. While the lawn adds a very nice framework to the landscape, that same lawn also can be cut (with a push mower) in seventeen minutes. Over the nine years at this location, we have steadily added and reduced plantings, expanded the deck, and added a deck awning. We have also added outdoor lighting that displays our rock ledge in the winter. The costs have been returned by our enjoyment of the property as well as the increase in the value of our home.

During the past three years, I watched drought distress my lawn and disease destroy most of it. Then I noticed that a friend of ours, Pam, always had a smirk on her face as she looked at my lawn. And *she* had a lovely green lawn. Finally, I took her advice on the correct products for our local soil and—*boom!*—my lawn turned around. I learned that I was buying the wrong fertilizers and insect and disease controls. I needed the Colorado fertilizers and controls but had been using the Michigan fertilizers and controls. I also learned that I was watering way too much.

If you do not have a Pam in your life and you want to know more about lawn care, your friendly county agricultural extension agent is the person to ask. He or she will send you free pamphlets with detailed procedures on how to create a great landscape with minimum upkeep. Your friendly librarian is another excellent resource. Shop at garage sales for hoses, edgers, and tools. Find a local nursery that mixes fertilizer for your locale. (That's the cheapest way to go because the bag will contain the correct amount of nutrients and minerals for your locale. The big national fertilizer firms just give you the basics, not the extra good stuff.) Effort and time will improve your outdoor living area and save you money in the end.

Now my lawn is very close to being where it should be, and it is very green. My highest compliment was from my next-door neighbor Bob. Bob asked, "How do you keep your lawn so green?" I should have sent him to Pam, but instead I pretended I was an expert.

Be coachable and learn from others; it is a wise investment.

Utilities are another area in which you can save money in your home. Little leaks mean a lot of lost wealth. (This is the converse of our formula for wealth: Little leaks allowed to continue over time lead to financial discontent.) Find your utility company's Web site and discover how to search for the ways you are losing money. (By the way, if you do not have a computer, go to the library and explain your predicament to the librarian. You'll be an expert in no time.) Or call the utility company and have them send you a printed form.

One of the greatest losses of money is the result of infiltration—air leaks around windows and external doors. Hot air in the summer and cold air in the winter infiltrate our homes and drive up our cooling and heating costs. Try this little gem. The next time the wind is really blowing around your house, light a candle and move it around the window frame. If the flame flickers, it is caused by air coming through gaps. Do the same test for external doors. If you plug those air leaks, you are also plugging money leaks. Find out more from your utility company and your library. Plug, plug, plug.

In every area of building and grounds maintenance, I encourage you to discover the fun of stopping your income from unnecessary out-go.

Cleaning and Organizing

You might be saying, "Neil, I do not think you understand my situation. I am resonating with you on the get out of debt thing, but I do not have enough money to get out of debt and buy weather stripping for my windows, let alone lawn care materials and tools. I am trying to reduce debt."

Okay, you have your priorities in order. (Although temporary weather stripping [four or five years' duration] can be made from clean Styrofoam meat packages. Sanitize them thoroughly and cut small strips to plug gaps.) But you are looking for something you can do that will not cost money but will be productive in moving you toward the right side of the Not Wealth/Net Wealth Scale.

Even if you have ten thumbs, you can clean, inventory, organize, and eliminate. Everyone has a closet, a drawer, a garage, a basement, or a room where evil lurks. That is the place we throw things. We are afraid to visit that place without a stick because something may have come alive. There very well might be monsters in there.

Several years ago our "place" was the storage room in the lower level of our home. It had not been touched for five years. We would throw things in and run before the whole thing exploded. One day Margie, in a moment of weakness prodded by guilt, tackled the job. I was, thankfully, out of town on business. But Margie is much tougher than I am. (Women are usually tougher than men. Come on guys, admit it. Childbirth? I fall apart if I have the twenty-four-hour flu.)

Anyway, Margie had read a book that changed her thinking about our den of iniquity. She began by emptying the storage room and putting the items in the living room of the downstairs apartment. She sorted things into categories, and then tried to find a "home" for them. (For some reason, the bromide "a place for everything and everything in its place" did not energize Margie. But upon reading that things need a "home," she was energized.)

I came home from my trip and was amazed at several things:

- The storage room actually had a floor. I hadn't seen it in years.
- Oh, is that where my Christmas pizza went three years ago?
- Things we personally rejected had a financial value. For example: An Early American pitcher and bowl set was worth $50, a vase $35, a Victrola $75, a wood stove $125, a complete set of *Mother Earth News* magazines, $300.

It took another few weeks to finish organizing the remaining items and place them in their proper homes. What did it cost us to clean, organize, inventory, and eliminate the blight on our souls? Zip, zilch, nada, nothing. And we made money several ways:

1. We discovered things we could use.
2. We discovered "lost" items that we had planned to replace.
3. We were able to sell some of what we owned.
4. We got a tax deduction for giving some of our things to good organizations.
5. We were too busy to go shopping! Victory was ours.

Since that time we have ransacked two closets and the garage. We now know what we have and where it is. And some people say that miracles aren't happening today. Ha! What do they know? I have my home to prove them wrong.

NAKEDNESS IS NOT AN OPTION

Mark Twain once said, "Clothes do make the person. Naked people have very little influence in our society today." Clothing is a necessity of life. But just because something is a necessity doesn't mean you can't save money on it—and have fun with it.

Perhaps clothing is where our faith most visibly collides with the culture. I recently heard the following conversations at a party, and I am not making them up:

"She is a nice enough person, but her clothes are *soooo* last season!" You would have had to be there to hear the tone of the voice.

A friend named Pat was talking on the other side of the room. Pat became the conversation piece for another group. "Pat has a killer suit. Did you see Pat's suit? It is a killer: Pat looks dead in it."

You immediately think that the above comments were made by society-minded non-Christians. Think again. They were made by upper-middle-class, Bible-study-attending, born-again Christians. Perfect examples of believers sucked into the whirlpool of getting and having.

When I challenged one of the speakers, the response was brief embarrassment and a quick, defensive counterattack: "Well, we have to be a witness to those around us. A witness in this neighborhood must dress to the level of the people in the neighborhood. I was merely helping Pat be a better witness."

I simply stared at her. Good grief.

As the CMC, we are not often invited to the social events of the really rich or the apparently really rich. I am glad. However, some of us must, whether we like it or not, dress up in big boy or big girl clothes. That means for guys, a noose around the neck; for ladies, I understand the girdle is coming back.

Can we dress with flair and be fashionably "okay"? Sure. We can do better than that. We can show up looking mighty fine without going "bespoke." (*Bespoke* is a term of derision used in *The Millionaire Next Door*. It means that a few "gentlemen" have had the "good fortune" to be introduced to a special person.[2] That person tailors the gentlemen's clothes to exact personal measurements. The gentlemen have an intimate "relationship" with their $2,000 suits. Makes me wonder, how do you have a relationship with a suit? Do you have to be introduced? Do you have to wear your suit for the first time with your tailor as your chaperone?)

By contrast, when asked what was the highest price they ever paid for a suit, a multimillionaire responded with a figure too low for you to believe. One man summed it up: "The most, the very most I ever spent [for a suit] was $399." [3] Off the rack. JC Penney. Whatever happened to "bespoke?"

Margie buys her clothes on sale at Talbots. We love to add up the markdowns. She has a professional position. As a VP, she needs to set a standard, but that doesn't mean she needs to break the bank.

For the first few years of my practice, I dressed every day in suits: Polo, Hart, Hickey Freeman. They were all hand-me-downs. I would buy new ties to "freshen" the look. For the past eighteen months, I have, by choice, returned to my frugal/poor roots. I made sure my family had real needs met: Jodi's continuing education in Costa Rica, partial help with Matt and Kellie's down payment on a house, and Margie's restoration/recreation. But I lived as if we had little money. I paid attention to how we spent money.

One of the things I did was to make a conscious decision not to buy any clothes for one year. I almost made it. My waist would not cooperate: one pair of pants, one pair of golf shorts. But I went through closets, drawers, the basement, and the attic. Found great things.

Remember that moths do not give a tinker's rip if your suit is from JC Penney or is "bespoke." Barbed wired doesn't care what kind of suit it tears, nor does your neighbor's terrier. The fashion industry preys upon men and women who want the newest styles. You might want to be more stylish when you are out of debt and your Net Wealth Scale is in proper balance. In the meantime, buy things that work with other things you already have in your wardrobe.

The key is the classic look, not trends. Can't you just hear the groans of the beautiful people, "How bourgeois!" On the other hand, one of my richest friends wears the same thing to every business meeting and social function: a green sports coat, plaid shirt, striped tie, tan pants, and shined loafers. He is not impressed with clothes.

A 2001 *Wall Street Journal* article titled "Cheapskate Chic" mentioned that there is an artform to blending labeled clothes with articles from discount stores.[4] If it works in NYC, it can work in your locale. Most of your acquaintances cannot tell whether your purse or briefcase is expensive. Don't tell them. Oh, please do buy clothes on sale—if the sale is legitimate. But pretend that you paid full price, and use the difference appropriately (ideally to pay off debt).

Shop smart. Better yet, de-clothe your closets; give some clothes away, see what you have, combine things, and make it work. If you need to gain weight (I can't imagine anybody feeling that pressure), do it. If you need to lose weight (ah, now I am on more comfortable ground), do it.

Clothing was one of the reasons I admired Jimmy and Rosalynn Carter. They started their presidency on the right foot as far as I was concerned. For the presidential inaugural ball, Rosalynn wore a dress she already owned; she had bought it the previous year. Compare that to Nancy Reagan who sported a brand-new, one-of-a-kind dress for the Reagans' first presidential inaugural ball. The price tag was a nifty $15,000.

Get a grip: Expensive clothes have no relationship to the status of being truly rich.

As an RCEO you must treat your household finances as you would a *properly* run business. Remember that a business has a goal of serving a *real* (as opposed to an imagined) need. The goal of your family business is to serve your family well. Better stated: Drive costs down and fun up! So have a plan, execute it, and watch your money grow.

STEPS TOWARD SHREWD

- Every home needs a Residential CEO if it is to become a wealthy home.
- $LT + E(T) + A^2 = FC^{10}$: *Little Things done Excellently over Time and Applied Appropriately equals Financial Contentment to the Tenth Power.*
- Your first steps as an RCEO are to set up an Information System and a Research and Development System.
- Next, pay attention to the thirteen divisions of your home, particularly building and grounds, cleaning and organizing, and clothing purchases.
- Treat your house like a properly run business—and have fun!

Strategizing Your Employment

My second career has been very interesting. It has focused on helping men and women achieve success in their jobs or in transitioning to a new job. One of my more nonastute observations is that many men and women are stuck in dead-end careers. They need to leave their present occupations. Most of them acknowledge that fact. And most of them stay right where they are.

Ninety percent of those who stay in bad situations say they are victims of money. They are stuck with debt, mortgages, car loans, private school costs, a lifestyle they must support, and so on. They cannot *afford* to risk a transition. In my mind they are in the bondage of money.

As we discussed in chapter 10, you simply must have an economically productive household, whatever stage of life or family you are in. (Again, Thomas Stanley and William Danko use this phrase well in their book *The Millionaire Next Door.*) You also need to be aware of the true cost of your work and then decide if it is bringing the financial wealth you think it is! Take a look at what work is really costing you.

YOUR AFTER-TAX DOLLARS ARE ALL YOU HAVE

According to the U.S. Bureau of Labor Statistics, in 2002 the average worker in the United States made $35,734.[1] This works out to $2,978 per month or $687 per week. However, Arthur Average does not receive $687 per week. There is the little matter of taxes to pay, such as federal tax, Social Security, and state and local income tax. *Ka-ching!* Oh, I almost forgot, Arthur probably owns his home and pays property tax. That should be figured into our tally. For convenience, let's assume that his tax bill is $156 per month.

$687 Gross income per week
− $156 Taxes
$531 Net Income (40 hours)

We are down to a little over $13.28 per hour. Gulp, yes, Arthur, there is more.

Getting ready for work 1 hour x 5 days per week:	5 hours per week
Commuting to work 1 hour x 5 days:	5 hours
Shopping and cleaning, washing, ironing clothes:	2 hours
Decompressing from work 1 hour x 5:	5 hours
Thinking/Talking about work 1 hour x 7:	7 hours
Total time:	24 hours

40 + 24 = 64 hours or $8.30 per hour
($531 after-tax dollars divided by 64 hours is equal to $8.30 per hour)

That figure is 49 percent of our original stated hourly wage. So our real net wage is $332 per week.

Now if that begins to attract your attention, I bet you can't wait to add in sales tax (in Colorado in 2003: 6.4 percent), and if we buy $10,000 worth of goods per year, that means we will pay an additional $640 per year or $12 per week. Can you believe it? But we are not finished.

Yes, there is more. Can you guess what it is? Gasoline tax! Doesn't add up to much, does it? Let's say you drive 13,000 miles per year and you get 20 miles to the gallon. That is a total of 650 gallons of gas. The tax is 40¢ per gallon or $260 per year or $5 per week.

Arthur's net/net/net weekly wage is $315 per week, not the $687 he has embedded in his financial brain lobes. While these figures should make all of us uneasy, it should also help us to understand why the checkbook is seldom (if ever) full.

If Arthur keeps the $687 figure in mind as he shops, he is in trouble because, somehow, some way, he is going the wrong way. How could that be? Here is the truth for Arthur: He and his family should shop with the idea that his after-tax salary is $315 per week, not $687. With that reality in mind, he will be much more sober and careful in his trips to the mall. The best news is that Arthur has information to share with his family to enlist their support. Figures do not lie; even teenagers can understand them.

What is the purpose of money? Why do we trade our life energy for money? Is it a fair trade? As Joe Dominguez and Vicki Robin ask in *Your Money or Your Life,* "Are you making a living…or a dying?"[2] If you are "making a dying" (a circular movement of ever-continuing work, exhaustion, and recovery for the sake of money), perhaps it is time to reflect on another strategy.

The Trap Facing Married Couples with Kids

Popular wisdom states that to live well today you must have a second income from a spouse's job outside the home. If one spouse is maxed out in terms of employment, it stands to reason that the other spouse should create income. After all, the checkbook must be served. The culture, which is always encouraging *more,* offers its support to this strategy. Our dual-income married friends tell us that they need two incomes just to make expenses. They are barely making it now; what would happen if one of them dropped out of the work force?

More money is never enough. The simple truth is that the less you spend, the more you have. *In order for normal CMCers to become wealthy, it is imperative that someone implement the spend-less plan and guard the back door of income out-go.* The savings realized on a home and associated expenditures are a key means to Financial Confidence and Financial Independence.

No, it is not the woman's automatic role to stay at home. I have taken a lot of time off from my practice to write this book. Reading, researching, interviewing, thinking, writing, editing, and frustration require a lot of time. But I was able to work from home. The Residential CEO (RCEO) deal was my job.

It is very difficult to have an economically productive household if both spouses work outside the home. (Unless there are no children in the home, chores are handled equally, and each spouse loves their job. Then it can work. But I am nervous about it.) Don't believe me? Okay, let's get after that two-incomes-are-a-given-in-today's-world view.

Larry Lifestyle is employed full time and makes $56,000 per year. Larry's spouse, Lee, does not work outside the home. Larry and Lee feel that what they have is not "enough." They are afraid of something happening to Larry's job. They feel they need more—more security, more money, but essentially, more stuff. And, oh yes, something for the Lord!

Let's say that Lee gets a 20-hour-per-week job that pays $12.50 per hour. Nice money, good hours. That is $250 per week or $1,000 per month or $12,000 per year. (Yes, I know that it really is $13,000 over 52 weeks, but with kids, holidays, sickness, and vacation, Lee will work only 48 weeks; part-timers usually do not have benefits.)

Larry and Lee figure they will be set for life and happy as clams if Lee could earn $12,000 per year. After all, $68,000 is very close to $70,000, and a *lot* more than $56,000. At least, that is what Larry and Lee's thinkers tell them.

To quote Zig Ziglar: "That is stinkin' thinkin'. You need a checkup from the neck up." But Lee thinks $12,000 would really help. *We could be out of debt and increase our lifestyle in a very short period of time. This job* *means that our income would jump to almost $70,000. The answer to our dreams. I'm going to do it!* (No, Lee, don't do it…yet. Please plan, Lee.)

That means that all of Lee's income will be kicked into the next tax bracket, in this case 25 percent for federal. Oh, and then there is state income tax of 5 percent (unless you reside in one of the "Lucky Seven").[3] And don't forget your share of Social Security and Medicare: 7.65 percent. Hmm, the tax bite appears to total 37.65 percent. Some of us are even fortunate to live in a community that charges local tax, but we will forgo that possibility to keep things simple. So, what does the grim reaper do to the bottom line?

The math: $12,000 x 37.65% = $4,518. Subtracting that sum from $12,000 gives us the new salary reality: $7,482. The grim reaper carries a very large tax scythe.

Well, even $7,482 will really help. Not as much as $12,000, but it is still positive. I'll do it! No, Lee, don't do it…yet. Please, Lee, plan a little more. Consider the costs associated with a new job. Perhaps you thought you had *no* expenses to consider? Silly you.

1. Commuting 5 miles one way = 10 miles round trip x 5 days = 50 miles per week x 4 weeks = 200 miles every month or 2,400 miles per year. The true cost, however, is $69 per month or $828 per year (2,400 x $0.345 [cost per mile according to U.S. government]). Part of what it takes to make the big bucks.

2. And, Lee, please do not use the expensive parking. You should walk the extra three blocks, or your salary will go down more. And don't even think about getting a ticket on your way to work. It is not the cost of the ticket but the insurance uptick that will kill you.

3. Clothing. *True, it is only a job in a day care* (a very expensive day care to pay Lee $12.50 an hour), *but a person can't just wear old things. I'm going to be good and cap my clothing expenditures at a max of $20 per month or $240 per year. But now that we are making almost $70,000, I can afford to look a little nicer.*

4. Lunches? *Every Friday, I will reward myself by going out to lunch. It is only once per week, and after all, we are making almost $70,000. The other four days I will make lunch. I am a good girl!*

5. Commuting revisited. *Well, we were going to get a new car anyway; this just sort of speeded up the process. But we can afford it if we make almost $70,000 per year. The payments* must *be within our budget. I wonder if we should check into leasing. They say you can get more car for less money and lower payments.*

6. Lunches revisited. *I know that we discussed this earlier, but I was too idealistic. Who has time to make them? Besides, there is a fabulous deli around the corner. And the entire gang goes there. Okay, Okay. I will bring my lunch two times a week and eat out three times a week.* ($8 average lunch expense x 3 days per week = $24 x 4 weeks = $96 per month = $1,152 per year.)

7. Coffee. Lee is not one of those big spenders—no lattes. Lee does like a grande Starbucks to get going: $1.55 (at least it is not the $3.50 that *some* people spend every morning!) x 5 days per week = $7.75 x 4 = $31 per month = $372 per year. *A drop in the bucket for people of our stature.*

8. Babysitting. *Grandma Margie loves our kids to death! And, since she loves to bake, she can make cookies for the kids while she's at it. (If she really loved us, she would cook dinner, but I don't want to push.) Cost: $0.* (In your dreams...) *I am stunned. Grandma Margie was too busy. (Doing what, I ask you?)*

9. Babysitting revisited. *But good old Grandma Marti can never get enough of the grandkids. She would die to keep Billy 10 hours a day, 5 days a week, and be there when Sally and Tally get home from school. I will leave a little list of things she could do around the house while Billy is napping. No sense in her not being productive. She does love us SOOO much! Is there any reason she couldn't get dinner started? "Grandma Marti, what do you mean, 'Over my dead body'?" Well, the ungrateful...that hurts! Well, at least I get a*

discount for putting Pumpkin in day care. Maybe she will meet a nice rich Christian young man. You can't tell about these things. Fortunately, we are at an income level that can handle this pothole. $25 per week x 4 = $100 per month x 12 = $1,200 per year.

10. Fatigue. At times Lee will have a hard day and will be allergic to cooking. Okay, let's build that into the plan. Twice a month. There, that sounds realistic. Fast food. No gourmet: $20 average family dinner expense x 2 = $40 per month or $480 per year. (Keep on dreamin'...) *We could afford more, but we want to be careful.*

11. Fatigue revisited. Larry says, "Honey, you really look bushed. Let's just go out to eat tonight. Burger King is too noisy and will give you a headache. Let's go to Marigold. We deserve it, after all, we are making..." $40 per week x 4 = $160 x 12 = $1,920 per year.

12. Fatigue costs continued. *There is just so much that needs to be done. (If Grandma would just get off her lazy duff, I wouldn't have this burden to bear.) Okay, we need a better vacuum so I can be much more efficient, and the new recessed microwave will let me cook faster and use less energy. They have a cleaning service that will actually pick up and deliver clothes to your door. It costs a little more, but after all, we are making... Come to think of it, maybe we shouldn't buy that vacuum. Mary told me about this fabulous home cleaning service. They are really good, bonded and very reasonable. I even think they do lawn care. After all, that is normal for people who make almost $70,000 per year.*

13. Guilt. *Okay, Pumpkin isn't getting as much of me as he used to. He can get two more DVDs each month from Blockbuster.* Hmm...$250 per year.

14. Lee probably should try to itemize the things that are no longer bought on sale, the use of coupons, and the increase in conven-

ience foods, but who has the time to count that? (From dreams to nightmares…)

15. *You know, I would feel so much better if I had a cell phone. Then I could keep in touch with the kids and have something in case of an emergency. And we can make all of our long distance calls on the cell phone to save money. After all…* $30 per month x 12 = $360 per year.

There is no secret here: Expenses always rise to meet income, and if corporations and advertisers have their way with you, expenses will rise to exceed income. That is where the profit is.

You want to add up those costs? No, I didn't think you did. It is obvious that they will be more than the second spouse earns.

Clue: If the second spouse sees himself or herself as a CEO of the home and takes on the job of making it an economically productive household, the world will be his or her lobster! (I know the proper word is *oyster,* but I like lobster a lot better.) The money saved by being efficient will be tax-free income that stays home. The money lost by employment and being nonefficient will be taxed as well as gone.

Calculate the real number of hours worked for a paycheck: Getting ready for work, shopping for work attire, traveling to and from the cleaners, standing in line at the cleaners, washing and ironing work clothes, traveling to and from work, parking, thinking and talking about work or work relationships/politics, buying snacks, gifts, and Girl Scout cookies from a coworker, participating in office pools. Calculate the unnecessary spending associated with work: compensation spending because you're too tired to cook, paying more for things because you're too tired to compare prices, buying at full price because you're too rushed to wait for a sale, taking manufacturer's recommendations at face value because you're too tired *and* too rushed to experiment.

Lee yells, "Stop it; this is depressing. Where are we?" $6,800 for expenses related to our job. Let's subtract that from the amount left over after the tax bite. $7,482 minus $6,800 = $682. Lee could have done better by staying home and buying into my Residential CEO Plan (RCEOP).

This brings me to my Red Letter Caveat about becoming an RCEO: The purpose of not having two incomes is so one person can guard the back door and stop the leaks in your financial system. If you join a bowling/tennis/golf/bridge league, have neighbors over for coffee, and solve your church's problems, you may be creating home problems.

Next is my Bright Red Letter Caveat: Though it is almost never economically better for a spouse to work outside the home, it can be important from an *emotional standpoint.* Many stay-at-home spouses feel a need to get out and connect with the marketplace as their children age and become more firmly entrenched in school (or maybe a few years before!). Couple that reality with the fact that stay-at-home spouses are viewed negatively by most of the culture, and there is a serious recipe for depression and a loss of self-confidence.

It might be important for a spouse to work outside the home for fulfillment. If this is true, remember our maxim: Win/Win or No Deal. Keep hammering at it until both of you feel heard and a winning strategy is in place.

That fulfillment might be found in a volunteer situation. It depends on the leading of the Lord and what will create the most energy and productivity in the spouse. For example, if the spouse is very talented with colors, patterns, shapes, and forms, it might make sense to volunteer at an interior design firm or help families decorate their new Habitat for Humanity homes.

Or it might make sense for a spouse to join the work force. The kids are in school and the job can be flexible, fun, and fruitful, but be home in time to connect with your kids. Or it might make sense to enter the work force when little Billy finally trails off to the army or college or correctional school.

If you are a DINK (Double Income, No Kids), try to live on one salary and save for a major down payment on a home or for retirement. Most DINKs do not plan and therefore live on both salaries. Consequently, when they become SIWKs (Single Income with Kids), life takes on a much more somber tone. When older DINKs become LINKs (Little Income, No Kids), life could be less than they might wish.

Every person will have a different story. But the procedure for developing and employing *the* right strategy remains the same: If you're married, get on the same page with your spouse by praying, talking, what-ifing, respecting the fears and concerns of your spouse, and most of all, making sure that Win/Win or No Deal applies. Take your time. The right win/win solution does not appear overnight. No matter where you are in life, be alert to what your work is costing you and giving you. Make choices that move you toward true riches.

STEPS TOWARD SHREWD

- Be aware of the actual expenses that are involved with your work.
- If you are married with kids, *strongly* consider having one spouse at home full time. It makes more economic sense than a second job.
- For some spouses, it may make emotional sense to work outside the home.

12

Steak for the Price of Hamburger

The secret to significant food savings is at hand. Significant savings? You bet! Let's say the average family will spend several hundred dollars a week at the grocery store (including personal and household items). Let's say it is $300 per week or $15,600 per year, which totals just under $400,000 over twenty-five years. On grocery store stuff! If you could save just 5 percent, the total would be $20,000! I want you to save between 25 and 40 percent! Do the math. That ought to make your little heart speed up a bunch. (More good news: This return on investment is in the premium form of *after-tax* dollars.)

In this chapter you will learn how you can save between 25 and 40 percent on grocery store expenditures. The goal is to deliver good nutrition and good taste to each member of your family for $2 or under per person per day. If you can do it for less money, so much the better. That would be your basic breakfast, lunch, snack, and dinner—all-inclusive. (FYI: Billions of people live on much less than $1 per day for everything.)

Yes, you do have to remember your Table Manners. Yes, you do have to know how to cook a little better than you do now. Yes, everyone must be on board. You have had a clear-the-air talk with your family, haven't you? Residential CEOs need support if they're going to become wealthy. Now let's look at those two keys to food savings: shopping and becoming a frugal chef.

SHOPPING

In my role as RCEO, I had to do the grocery shopping. My goal was to be efficient, quick, and ruthless in ensuring the stores made as little profit from us as possible. I honed our food shopping to razor sharpness. The key was making a plan based on what low-cost items were available, not on what we were in the mood for.

Newspaper food advertisements are your first line of defense in accumulating significant food savings. Keep two or three store flyers at the most and throw the rest away. Make sure you do not travel too far from home since the additional transportation expenses may negate your grocery savings.

The day the grocery flyers arrive, take out a sheet of paper, a red marker, a pen, and a small calculator. Look at the loss leaders, the items that grocery stores will sell at a loss to get us into their store. Almost without fail, loss leaders will be attractive features for your menu planning. When loss leaders are combined with coupons at double-coupon stores, you can save big.

If possible, make arrangements to shop without the kids. And do not enter a grocery store when you are hungry. Avoid the samplings offered by taste testers. Once the tasty treats enter your mouth, you will probably not be able to resist the sales pitch.

Notice the prices of all the things you buy regularly. Compare the typical costs and notice when those things go on sale. Become an expert in minimizing the profits of grocery stores. This will move you toward the right side of the Not Wealth/Net Wealth Scale.

Develop a list of every item you use and write down a price for each item. Then take a pocket calculator with you when you shop so you can tell when there is a good sale on an item. Put any extra storage space you have to good use by buying in very large quantities.

Do not expect to have everything in order right away. But within a few months you should expect to see progress—progress that can be tallied financially.

For you it might take twenty to twenty-five minutes a week for a few weeks to review these two or three supplements and discover their secrets. After that, probably no more than twelve to fifteen minutes a week. The flyers have so much information that you may feel overwhelmed. Most of what is listed in them is listed at the regular price. But amazing things will happen: You will know your prices. After three or four weeks of reading these flyers, you will notice that salmon is usually $4.99 at one store and $3.99 at another. That is a dollar. Dollar savings add up.

The chant at your friendly neighborhood grocery is: Confusion of customers leads to profits for us. So many choices, so little time; and each and every cashier has been trained to be very nice. "Have a good day, Mr. Atkinson." Your defense is knowledge. Knowledge of the true sales and knowledge of your true needs. The confusion will dwindle away as your knowledge expands week by week over time.

My average visit to the supermarket nets at least a 35 percent savings. That savings comes from planning meals ahead of time, shopping when I am not hungry, shopping when there are very few customers in the store (the worst time to shop at a grocery store is between 4:00 and 7:00 in the afternoon), buying loss leaders, buying only what is really on sale (as opposed to a sucker "sale"), and buying a lot of an item when it is really on sale. The savings are tax-free. Gourmet meals. Margie is a happy wife.

Here's hoping that a bunch of your enthusiasm and ingenuity connect with your financial reality. Regular grocery savings of 30–50 percent are easily possible even if you do not live near a store that does double coupons.

Many of my busy friends are reading this and groaning, *I don't have the energy to do that sort of thing!* Many of my well-to-do friends are reading this and shaking their heads in dismay: *What a waste of time!* Think so? In *The Millionaire Next Door,* Thomas Stanley and William Danko tell of the husband who gave his wife $8 million worth of stock in his company. She smiled and went back to clipping her coupons.[1]

The Deception of Buying in Bulk

You might be saying right now, "Oh no, Neil is telling me I have to become a coupon king (or queen), eat store brands, tofu, and go to seven different stores before I buy anything. Shoot, Neil! I just go to warehouse stores and do *all* my shopping there. Everyone knows they have the best prices. Really, I am set here."

Did you hear that whooshing sound? That was your money being vacuumed out of your wallet. The warehouse-club boys are good and very profitable. The reason is, "Whatever the market will bear." You be the market, they be the bear.

I just read in a magazine, in fact, that a great way to budget is to buy everything from warehouse stores. At least, that was the case for a reporter who did not bother with research. Discounters want you to believe that you can save on everything by buying in bulk.

In one of my seminars, a young man, Jeff, challenged my cautionary mentality. He said that he had gone to a discount store and saved 36 percent. I like challenges. If I am wrong, I learn. If I am right, I gloat (in a humble, spiritual sort of way, of course).

So the next week I took my usual twelve minutes with the brightly colored food flyers of two stores. I usually look at a third, but I wanted to limit my options in the name of fair research. I scanned the supplements and circled in red the best buys around which I would build the menus for the week. As usual, I tried to plan our meals based on what was on sale, not on what I felt like eating at the moment. I decided on steak, chicken, and salmon for entrées, and selected eighteen other items. For the sake of comparison, I took a three-by-five card and wrote down each item with the best price from the two stores.

Then I visited the discounter to compare item for item. The discounter was lower on seven of the items. The two grocery stores were lower on the other twenty-one items. Total savings by going with the regular stores: 14 percent, which is a mind-boggling return on investment in today's stock market.

The truth is, you have to be alert when you go to discount stores. Here are just a few reasons why:

1. Discounters can save you money, but you must be alert.
2. Membership fees are a hidden cost and will offset your savings.
3. You will buy in bulk, so the chance of spoilage is greater.
4. You will see "great deals" on stuff not on your list, which encourages impulse buying. Translation? You will spend money you had not planned to spend.
5. You will face horrendous lines.
6. They have only 4,000 items in stock as compared to your normal supermarket's inventory of over 20,000 items.
7. You will probably have to travel out of your normal traffic route to shop at discount clubs. Translation? You will likely spend more money just traveling to and from the discounter.
8. Discounters will not accept coupons. You do not need a translation for that.

Discounters *can* save you money, *if*…and that's a great big fat IF:

- You do not live too far away from the store.
- You know how specific prices compare to other stores (bring a calculator).
- You go with a plan and buy the plan and no more!
- You get out with your wallet still intact.

Here are a few household items I bought at a discounter: Curél lotion (the only thing that works for Margie—you think I am going to mess with that?), mouthwash, Dove and Irish Spring bath soaps, a few vitamins, shaving cream, one pair of pants, and one pair of golf shorts. You can get significantly better prices on cheese, butter, and eggs at most discounters. Unfortunately, you must buy these items in bulk, and again, spoilage is a consideration unless you can freeze them.

Notice what is *not* on the list: dishwashing liquid, laundry detergent, dishwasher soap, toothpaste, toilet paper, paper towels, tissues, and so on. Grocery stores have real savings on certain things at certain times. When those times occur, invest like crazy. Buy a year's supply. At all other times, keep yourself and your wallet away from there.

You might still make mistakes. The first year of our marriage, I began practicing the strategy of buying certain things in bulk. I found my favorite shaving cream on sale. In the big size no less. I put four cans in the storage area. Six months later I still had three of the cans. We moved to California that same month. Every single can burst in the move. Oops.

A Surefire Investment

So here are my tips for saving money when you go grocery shopping:

1. Remember the Law of Demand and Supply: Never let Demand (your children's desires) fuel your meal selection. Let Supply (what you plan, buy on sale and have on hand) be the means by which meals are prepared. Otherwise, a second law, the Law of Supply and Demand, will eat your lunch. Here is that not-so-pretty picture: My supply is low, but the demand is high. Therefore, I must buy the demanded goods when the price is right for the grocery store, but wrong for my family.

2. Remember that the SOE (Save on Everything) principle gives the best return on investment.

3. Let the two or three stores in your neighborhood tell you what you are going to eat for the next week. Always read the flyers and plan your menu *only* on what is truly on sale.

4. Compare flyers from the stores to see what is the best value. Compare at least two but no more than three stores. No sense wearing yourself and your transportation out.

5. Clip coupons, organize your coupons, and be alert to double and triple coupon sales. I was a coupon snob until I read a blurb in Mary Hunt's *Cheapskate Monthly* newsletter that used that phrase. But be careful that you only use coupons for things you and your family need and use.

6. Beware of discount stores. Do not automatically assume they are your one-stop shopping place. You might buy too much, and you might buy things not on your list.

7. Make a shopping list and a map of the aisles in the store where the items are located. Only buy what is on your list.

8. Develop a price list. Research prices as you shop. Use a calculator and record what you see. This will save you time in the long run.

9. Over time you will have moved to alertness regarding the best sales. Buy as much as you can afford when you don't need it.

10. Shop on a full stomach.

11. Shop without the kids, if at all possible.

12. Pay attention to the prices entered by the cashier because he or she can make mistakes.

13. Note your savings, and use the money to get rid of debt or add to your accumulation fund.

Following these guidelines will save you as much as 40 percent or more every time you shop.

Review the last item in the list above. You have not saved anything if you channel the money you didn't spend at the grocery store into your lifestyle. Lifestyle leads you back to the starting line, the left side of the scale, the Not Wealth side.

BECOMING A FRUGAL CHEF

Let us review the Table Manners: coachability, enthusiasm, ingenuity, and toughness. You can do it. You need to be challenged. So the next thing you need to do is become a certain type of chef. No, I am not insulting you. You are probably an excellent cook. But as a part-time employee outside the home, you didn't have the time to become a frugal chef. Today is a different matter.

(*Note:* If you are still working outside the home, I want to encourage you to follow this plan as well. Food costs are a killer for single people and working couples because of the fatigue factor. Eating out and picking up convenience meals costs at least 100 percent more than eating the same meal at home. If refraining from eating out seems too difficult right now, start with a small pilot project: Bring your lunch three days a week, or be intentional about eating leftovers for dinner on Monday. Then project those savings for twelve months. Christmas will be a cinch this year!)

So what is a frugal chef? It is someone who can make *phenomenal* meals much less expensively than regular home-cooked meals. Over time you will prepare better meals than you can get at most restaurants. Yes, you read that correctly. While you may never be a Dominique or a Michael, you can become a great chef. You can use the same stove that came with the house, the same pots and pans, the same knives that you have right now. No further expenditures are necessary. It is the technique, not the utensils, that make a great frugal chef!

Start with meals that *you* enjoy and that your family at least tolerates. Rework them; re-create them. How can you prepare them more inexpensively, present them more appealingly, and create more taste? Think. Check the library. Watch Emeril on the Food Network. "BAM! Let's kick it up a notch." Get picture cookbooks. Talk to friends. Experiment. Laugh at your failures, learn from your successes. Too much jalapeño made an early version of my trout paté unpalatable. On the other hand, using canned evaporated milk instead of half-and-half significantly reduced the cost of a butternut squash gratin and actually improved the texture.

Gradually expand to apply the same principles for each of your family members' favorite meals. You will quickly see that many spices overlap, and inexpensive ones can sometimes be used in dishes that call for more expensive ones. No recipe in a cookbook is from God. If you don't have one or two items, either ignore them or substitute something you already have or like better—for example, brining chicken in a one-to-one mixture of sugar to salt in two quarts of water instead of soaking it in buttermilk and butter.

Life will be good. Meals will be great. And inexpensive. For example, last week Margie and I spent a total of $11.15 for fourteen dinners (7 days x 2 people = 79¢ per person per dinner). Our dinners consisted of:

- hickory-smoked trout paté on oven-crisped cookie-size tortilla rounds. (I caught the trout.) Cost: $1.50;
- hickory-smoked whole chicken with leek and cilantro stuffing; bread stuffing with garlic, onion, corn, and tomatoes; and butternut squash gratin made with Gruyère cheese. (I didn't catch the chicken.) Cost: $3.50;
- grilled sirloin steak and vegetables. (Steak bought with red sticker on it; vegetables picked from our garden.) Cost: $2.25;
- leftover hickory-smoked chicken with potato pancakes. Cost: 45¢;
- fresh onions, tomatoes, zucchini salsa on black beans. (Vegetables from our garden.) Cost: 45¢;
- salmon omelets. (I caught the salmon.) Cost: $1.25; and
- pan-fried pork steak cutlets served on red lettuce with a lemon vinaigrette. Cost: $1.75.

I realize you may not be able to catch your own fish, but you should be able to maintain a small garden. Even most apartment-dwellers can raise vegetables and herbs in containers. You'll be amazed at the money this will save you. The sirloin steaks and thin pork steak cutlets I bought were red-sticker meats, bought the last day they could be sold in a grocery store meat department. Therefore, the price of each item was reduced.

"Aha! Gotcha!" you say. "You admitted that you buy meat that is old and tainted."

I did no such thing. I bought marked-down meat the last day it could be sold in the store. I had a good talk with my friendly neighborhood butcher. She explained the process to me. "We only have this meat for four days, and then we must throw it away! (Did you read that? They throw it away!) The meat that has a red sticker on it *must* be sold by the next day. A little incentive. I buy it all the time. My freezer is full of it."

I started buying the red-sticker items and noticed no difference in quality, taste, or appearance. But I needed stronger data to prove that red-sticker meat was as good as no-sticker meat. The test would come when I had a few of my "foody" friends for dinner. They loved what I cooked for them! Total cost of entertaining six, including Margie and me: $15.62.

Monster cookings will save time and money. If you face a busy week, spend the previous Saturday morning preparing and freezing several meals. (Aren't you glad you cleaned out the freezer?) If you are grilling a chicken for guests, grill two and freeze one.

Lest you think we always eat gourmet, let me reassure you that very easy meals can also be fun and cheap. And, no, you don't have to spend four bucks on a diet TV dinner. For example, yesterday I had a bowl of cereal with soy milk for breakfast, along with two glasses of water. For lunch I had tuna with mustard and horse-radish sauce and garden vege-tables. As an afternoon pick-me-up, I had a carmel-coffee soy drink, and then for dinner we had grilled chicken with garden vegetables, sour cream, and guacamole, and cake for dessert. Not only was this healthier than your standard processed fare, it was inexpensive—and we even had a few leftovers from dinner for lunch the next day.

You do not have to live on popcorn for a month. (Although, that is a good snack, and in a pinch it can do well for dinner.) Shopping and cook-ing wisely will open up all sorts of frugal options.

I learned this firsthand long ago. My dad was a farm boy—one of seventeen children. He thought the crust of bread was the best part of the loaf and wanted his pancakes burned and greasy. (He loved Margie's homemade stew so much that he gave her the ultimate compliment: "Margie, is this Dinty Moore stew?")

My dad cooked on Sunday nights when we were growing up. He often cooked a meal called "bread and milk toast." He would warm milk and toast bread. When things were ready, he would put warm milk, a piece of bread, a piece of toast, and a small amount of butter in a bowl. That was Sunday supper. We enjoyed it and managed to survive to eat another day.

You already know that breakfast for dinner is a great way to make food budgets get slimmer. In our financially poor years, we would have scrambled eggs and blueberry muffins for dinner twice a week. We enjoyed those meals, too.

What happens when your family does not like what you serve? You have at least two choices when it comes to feeding children and winning without spending too much:

1. You say, "My children will not tolerate most things. And that is my final answer." To paraphrase Marie Antoinette, "Let them eat nothing." After a little while, hunger produces new taste buds, the disdained things of the past become a repast in the present.

2. While you are working to tip the balance of the scale to the Net Wealth side, let the kids eat their favorite sandwich for dinner while you enjoy a different dish. For example, little Joey and little Muffie enjoy peanut butter and pickle sandwiches. You and your spouse enjoy liver. Let J and M be content with their sandwiches and milk. You have fed them a complete protein. They are happy. In the meantime, you munch your liver with delight. Delight, by the way, that is not punctuated with cries of distress and threats of calling social services because of food abuse. Everyone is happy; everybody wins. After you are solidly on the Net Wealth side of the scale, you can return to the Brussels sprouts discussion.

It is now your turn. The best shopping and cooking has yet to happen. You might have three very small successes and then something that is completely off the charts in saving money, getting value, and delighting your family.

STEPS TOWARD SHREWD

- Paying attention to your food shopping and consuming can save you a significant amount of money.
- Saving money on food takes ingenuity, but it can be fun!
- Enter any store with a plan of what you will buy (based on loss leaders), and stick to it.
- Remember the tips about discount stores and about wealth-promoting grocery shopping.
- Learn how to be a frugal chef who outperforms restaurant chefs.
- You can do this!

13

Buying a House

Here are two lies our culture wants us to believe: (1) having a mortgage isn't that big a deal, and (2) a house is the same thing as a home. We also hear a lot of different opinions about what kind of house to buy as well as when and how to buy it. So here is some truth, some advice about buying a home, as well as a few creative ideas to consider.

GOING AGAINST THE GRAIN

For most middle-class Americans, a very long stretch of the road to wealth can be paved by owning a house debt-free. Now, you may be thinking, *Pay off the house? I can understand paying off credit cards, even automobiles. But interest on our house payment is the only income-tax break I have left! Who ever pays off their house mortgage?* People who are wealthy, that's who. No, I don't mean people who are wealthy and have the money to pay it off. I mean people who pay it off so they can become wealthy.

This does go against the grain. And right now, a few bankers are reaching for the Pepcid. Why, if people caught on to this truth, their profits would shrink. Poor babies. But *your* wealth would grow. What a concept!

The common advice is that you should always keep your house payment low by having a thirty-year mortgage, use the interest for the tax break, and invest the difference left over from your smaller payment. Once again, let me be perfectly clear: I believe, for the CMC, the common advice has a bad aroma.

Having a fully paid-off home (has a really nice ring to it, doesn't it?) offers several advantages to having a mortgage.

1. The emotional payoff of knowing you have a home free and clear of debt is huge! *No* argument there.

2. Your home becomes a tool against the ravages brought about by supply and demand. For example, if the U.S. population increases, the need for housing will also rise. When the need for housing rises, so does the value of your home.

3. As your house payments become toast, that money can now be applied to other things, such as education or retirement.

There are two main reasons people give for not paying off their home: (1) tax break, and (2) investment opportunities. Tax break? Give me a break. Your tax deduction for interest is a silly reason for not paying off your home. Reasons for that thinking? Sure:

- Interest deductions lower your taxable income, not your taxes. That is not the same thing. Not even close.

- With today's lower interest rates and tax law changes (who knows what will happen tomorrow?), those interest dollars do not count for much against taxes.

- Those interest dollars move you in the wrong direction on the Not Wealth/Net Wealth Scale (as in, toward the start, not the finish).

Let's say you spend one dollar in interest and you are in the 25 percent tax bracket. That means that you will receive a tax refund of 25¢, but you have *lost* 75¢. Will this make you wealthy and the master of your money? Put another way: If you give me a dollar, I will be happy to give you back a quarter.

When it comes to investment opportunities, the argument goes something like this: A thirty-year mortgage typically means smaller monthly payments, so you should invest the money you "save" each month rather than using that money to pay your principal. You know who thought of this stupidity? The financial industry. You know who bought that stupidity? ME! Before I became shrewd.

Returns on the stock market since 1925 (before the Great Depression) have averaged around 11 percent. That is a lot of nice compound interest. Financial people tout this and state that the numbers are on their side. You cannot argue with numbers.

But you can ask questions. For example: How much of that return was the result of dividends? A little over 4 percent? Okay, another question. Are companies paying dividends these days? No? Why not? Because the companies will reinvest their earnings for your benefit. Do you smell an Enron here?

The error of people who say that it's best to keep a mortgage and invest the difference is that they *assume* that history will repeat itself *and* that you will be able to get out at the top of the market. They protect themselves with this disclaimer: "While future profits are not guaranteed, historically the stock market returns 11 percent." Okay. Will your financial person *guarantee, out of their own pocket,* that you will earn 11 percent? If so, check their financial statement, and then have them put it in writing. In addition, what do fees and commissions do to the real rate of return?

So having an eternal mortgage for the tax break and investment opportunities is not for the CMC.

INTEREST EVAPORATION LEADS TO GREAT WEALTH

We must rid ourselves of Devastating Debt and Decent Debt. (Most home loans fall under the umbrella of Decent Debt.) Essentially, debt is presumption. You presume you will be able to make the payments. A case could be made for borrowing money if you borrow only to pay for items that appreciate in value. Otherwise the debt deck is stacked against you. Having any debt means that you are heading back to the starting line of the scale. In other words, you are heading back to the Not Wealth side. Don't you hate it when you have to start over? So what does it look like to pay off your house? And why does it work? (I am suggesting that if you own a home, get an amortization schedule and review it every month. You will be amazed at what it costs to rent money to "buy" a home.)

Okay, KISMIF (Keep It Simple, Make It Fun!).

For the sake of illustration, let's say that you buy a house for $100,000. Your monthly mortgage is $1,000. (Humor me on these simple numbers. They clarify things for the math challenged.) But you pay...

Beginning Balance	Monthly Payment	Principal	Interest	Ending Balance
$100,000	$1,000	$50	$950	$99,950
$ 99,950	$1,000	$50	$950	$99,900
$ 99,900	$1,000	$55	$945	$99,855

After three months, it is easy to see that this is not progressing very well for you. But at this point, your banker is smiling and perhaps offering donuts and coffee every month.

What would happen if you "skipped" your second payment by paying an extra $50 toward the principal? (You do that by writing an extra check marked for "principal" and including it with your first payment.) Why, my friend, you would therefore not owe the $950 of interest that was due with the second payment. Voilà! You have not spent $950! What a great return on investment.

Beginning Balance	Monthly Payment	Principal	Interest	Ending Balance
$100,000	$1,050	$100	$950	$99,900

Therefore, we skip payment 2 and the interest payment of $950. The next payment made is payment 3:

$ 99,900	$1,050	$105	$945	$99,795

Therefore, we skip payment 4 and the interest payment of $945.

It comes down to this: The key to middle-class wealth is a fully paid-off house as soon as possible. The less money you have to pay to rent money to buy your home, the more money you will save over time, which means that you will be well on the road to mastering your money and becoming financially wealthy.

WHEN TO MOVE

Margie and I often find ourselves looking at other houses for the possibility of a move. (I promise you, we just happen to "find" ourselves in model homes and at the Parade of Homes. We are transported there by magic. One moment we are home with coffee, and the next we are in a new home.) We do not intend to buy, but we look once or twice a year.

Now that's strange. Margie and I are happy with each other. She assures me that she is not currently in the market for a Trophy Husband. (The relationship is, in Margie's terms, a 9.5. She can't think of anything wrong, but she knows there must be "something.") Our home is in a great location with an ideal floor plan for our lifestyle. A magnificent park over five miles in length is one block away. The views are to live for. Shopping is convenient. Our neighbors range from great to cordial. There is no downside to remaining where we are. Why, then, do we peruse open houses or model homes? I'll give you six reasons:

1. "Moving up" is the American way.
2. We start thinking about the "investment opportunities."
3. We get ideas about different landscaping or interior designs.
4. We get restless and want a "project."
5. Stupidity.
6. All of the above.

The truth is, sometimes it comes down not to the "having," but the "getting." It's a trap that is easy for any of us to fall into. Our internal makeup begins to lean toward accepting the brainwashing of our culture. We become bored, discontent, and dissatisfied, and we think that something "new" will fix all that internal mishmash. So before you get too deep into looking to buy a new house, consider the following:

1. A house is much more than a shelter or an investment. A house can also become a home that provides schooling, sanctuary, entertainment, and ministry. A house can become a home that is warm and inviting to all who enter.

2. The converse is also true: A house can just be a house, not a home. Many people own a house but do not have a home. You can tell as soon as you walk in their door; you're greeted by cold, sterile vibrations that are empty of warmth and welcome.

Do you want to buy a house? Would you be better off renting for a few more years, maybe moving from an apartment to a duplex? Run the numbers.

Consider a few things:

- The money and energy it takes to make a house function. In other words, you may be able to "afford" a house payment (barely), but can you afford the other costs that will envelop you?
- The cost of utilities: heating and cooling, electricity, water, wastewater, garbage collection, association fees, and so on.
- The cost of furniture; after all, you cannot live in an empty house.
- Equipment costs; if you are like me (and I know I am), you will need at least two, maybe three, grills: gas, charcoal, and fire-pit.
- Taxes that fund schools, streets, libraries, public services, property tax, and so on.
- Home maintenance and repair. Things break. Do you fix those things or does a professional (for additional money, of course)?
- "Yardening"—such as cutting, edging, raking, trimming, weeding, and fertilizing, all of which costs money.

- The cost of keeping up with affinity groups (the new Joneses)? Your neighborhood will set standards (e.g., lawn care). Do you want the looks that come your way by ignoring those standards? Do you like to be shunned? If not, be prepared to shell out money to toe the line.
- Continual upgrades of fences, equipment, and so on.
- I think you get the picture.

How to Buy a House

If you determine that, *yes,* this is the time to buy a house, remember to buy the right house (for you). After seven years of marriage, my son and daughter-in-law, Matt and Kellie, made the decision to buy a house. They chose less house than the kind mortgage folks said they could afford. Why? I promise you it wasn't because I gave them advice; they figured it out on their own. They wanted to live comfortably in that house, not under a financial strain that would have produced stress. They hoped that one of them would be able to stay home with children. That meant they would have to live on one income. They are accomplishing that goal and now have the world's cutest daughter.

Here are some other specific tips for First Timers who want to *carpe housem* (seize the house):

- Buy less than the mortgage people say you can afford.
- Remember that by law, the real-estate agent (unless he or she is a buyer's agent), works for the seller. Let's repeat that: The real-estate agent works for the seller. For example, in one case I know about, the real-estate agent did not point out that asbestos surrounded the exhaust duct of the air conditioner. I am not saying he did this intentionally; I am saying that you may be much better off being knowledgeable and hiring a professional inspector who works for *you.*

- Do not be impulsive; do your "hobbywork." (I would have said "homework," but some of you would have fainted at the thought.) Find three to five neighborhoods that would work for you. By *work* I mean are they located near good schools, shopping, and your place of employment? Do you feel comfortable there? Have you talked with people working in their yards? Would you want to live next door to them?

- Start with the idea that you will eventually have to sell the house. Make sure your house and location will be attractive to future buyers.

- Arrange your financing. If you have a good credit rating and a history of good employment and responsibility, the very best financing is from a relative. Offer the relative more than he or she could get from a CD, but 1 percent less than the interest from your mortgage people. You will want to provide your relative with mortgage documentation as well as copies of your life and disability insurance. These documents will protect him or her in case a calamity befalls you.

- The less money you must pay to "rent" money for your house, the better able you will be to master your money. Therefore, a high down payment and lower interest rate move you toward the finish line: assets, wealth, mastery.

- Do not fall in love with one home. Find several that will "work" as your first home. You will learn so much by owning your home that you will know exactly what to look for if you decide to buy another.

- Hire the best home inspector you can afford. Listen to him or her. Are there structural problems (read: bye-bye dollars) or cosmetic problems (needs paint, lawn and landscape are in terrible shape, etc.)? If the inspector says the former, back out of the deal. If he or she says the latter, renegotiate the price.

- If you wish to purchase a For-Sale-by-Owner (FSBO) home, remember this: Ostensibly (a big word—my editor will be so pleased), an FSBO should save you money. After all, the seller no longer has to pay a commission of 6 percent to an agent. Realistically, you *have* to do your hobbywork. Find out what comparable homes are selling for in your neighborhood (libraries will point you in the right direction). In all likelihood, the owners have done some major repairs (new furnace) and some cosmetic repairs (paint, etc.). Probe behind the paint to see if there is rot. Don't take the risk of selling or buying FSBO unless you do your research and you (and your spouse) feel comfortable with it!

A House Is Not a Home

Whatever you decide about renting, buying, or staying, remember that there is a big difference between a house and a home.

A house is where you find physical shelter. It is a project; a project that takes time and money. You can move into your first house with all the excitement in the world. There is so much to do and so much money to spend. Whether you buy, build, rebuild, decorate, redecorate, or just maintain, a house is a never-ending consumer of resources, both monetary and emotional. A friend of mine built his dream house with his wife, no expense spared; it had everything. On the very day that this couple moved into the house, they had the biggest fight of their marriage. Two years later the divorce was final. They built a house, not a home.

A home is much different than a house. A home is where you want to be not only because it offers physical shelter but because it offers sanctuary. Sanctuary means a place to find solace, comfort, excitement, laughter, challenge, and reality. You feel safe enough there that you do not have to *pretend* to be a human, you can actually *be* a human. You may laugh or cry, be angry or joyful, junk-talk or deep-talk. A home is where you want to be when you hear bad news. It is where you want to be to celebrate Christmas. It is where you want to be.

I grew up in a house. And for a long period in our marriage and family life, we had a house that was sometimes a home, or a home that was sometimes a house. Today, my family and I have a true home. That is God's fault; He has to take the responsibility. Took a lot longer to get there than books say it should. But God did it.

If you own a home, ask yourself whether you have a *house* or a *home*. Perhaps you are spending money on the wrong things. Instead of buying new furniture or doing home improvement projects, it may be advisable to invest in dinners, weekends, and other activities to keep your relationships authentic and growing. (As opposed to inauthentic and boring.)

As you look to buy a home, keep these definitions of *home* in mind:

1. *Home is where the wealth is.* As we learned in chapter 10, many separate economic entities make up a home. If a person owns the house in which a home is found, those entities will be seen as divisions that need to be managed. Taking care of those things will not only save you money, it will make your environment a caring, intentional one.

2. *Home is where the fun is.* It sounds simple, but it's true: You could have more money than you know what to do with and still not have a home. The person in front of you in the grocery line may not have one-sixteenth of your money, but she is going to a home that night because her family has fun. They discover new things that don't cost money. They are ingenious. They enjoy their favorite activities. Their fun creates a home.

3. *Home is where the heart is.* Ask yourself, Do we want to *have* a life, or do we want to *pretend* to have a life? More money is not the answer. Focusing life in the right direction is the answer. And that makes a home.

STEPS TOWARD SHREWD

- Having a *fully paid-off house* is the secret to middle-class wealth.
- Always buy less than the mortgage people say you can afford.
- Know when to move and how to buy a house.
- Wherever you decide to live—a house, an apartment, a duplex—invest yourself into making your *house* a *home.*

14

Your Transportation Can Make You Wealthy

The same truth of house buying applies to buying a vehicle: We fall into the trap of getting and having instead of focusing on what we already have. We buy more than we should. Our culture plays the same music over and over again, and our automatic internal response begins to throb:

- "Are we what we drive? Yes!"
- "Do we want our neighbors to think less of us? No!" (Think of the great *witness* we can have with our non-Christian neighbors by buying more car than we need or can afford!)
- "Do we dare inflict enduring emotional pain on our children by taking them to school in a loser car? No, we love our children! It is our sacred parental duty to have the best car we cannot afford."

How can an auto help your Net Wealth and hurt your Not Wealth?

First, never use the word *investment* in the same sentence with the word *automobile*. An auto is not an "investment." Investments are supposed to have a reasonable chance of increasing in value. If you buy a new car, your only, *only,* reality will be to watch your money go away, vamoose, skedaddle. An auto is either (1) an expense, or (2) a projection of our psyche *and* an expense.

Second, buy a preowned car from a trusted friend. Do this as seldom as possible.

Third, if you buy a car every three to five years (after all, those things do get dirty), use rented money to finance it, and then sell it for its depreciated price, you are living a lifestyle. You are hurrying toward Not Wealth. Buying and keeping a car that fits your personal criteria for the least amount of money is a steppingstone to wealth. An entrance on the freeway to Not Wealth/Net Wealth is called Auto Lane. The way to move to Not Wealth is to buy a new automobile every three or four years. The way to Net Wealth is to refrain from such purchases.

I know of a couple in Denver who has two cars with over 500,000 miles on them combined. Their cars are in great condition but have never been near an auto repair center.

Here is what that says to me: (1) they are good drivers, (2) one of them is a talented auto mechanic, and (3) they have saved a bundle of money. Their cars are an '87 Honda Civic and an '88 Oldsmobile 88. If this couple were "normal," they would have purchased six or seven vehicles in the last fifteen years. Let's assume they could pay cash for the cars. Let's also assume they bought new cars. Are you wincing at the thought?

Lots of dollars spent. Lots of dollars up in smoke.

It makes much more economic sense to purchase a two- or three-year-old preowned (read: used) auto with low mileage (still may have time left on the factory warranty) than to buy new. The less you pay in depreciation, the greater your chances of moving toward Net Wealth. The more you pay in depreciation, the greater your chances of falling on your financial face.

Your transportation can make you wealthy if you avoid buying new cars and buy very few cars during the course of your lifetime. However, if you are reading this chapter, there is a strong chance that you are looking for another vehicle. If that is true, I urge you to apply shrewdness to this purchase.

Let's look at how to figure out what you want, why you want it, and how much you should pay to get it.

Selling Your Old Car

Okay, you want a new car. No, you have determined you *need* a new car. This is not a *want,* nor is it a *lust;* it is a genuine, bona-fide *need.* But you do not have the money to pay cash. No? Consequently, you would also *need* to borrow the money. Which side of the Not Wealth/Net Wealth Scale are you moving toward: own or owe?

Let a thought ride to your rescue: You can sell your old auto. You know better than to let the dealer steal it from you. You know you should sell it to a private party. Believe me, it is not a hassle. It is relatively easy. That statement is true if the car is priced right and it is in good to outstanding condition. Why not invest a little time in it to bring top dollar? Sure, I knew you would see the wisdom of that thought.

A car in excellent or outstanding condition will bring the best return on investment. The condition of a preowned vehicle is classified as outstanding, excellent, clean, average, or rough. Do not assume that your car is in excellent condition just because you have been the owner. (For more detailed information as to your vehicle's condition and its worth a visit to www.edmunds.com and www.kbb.com [Kelley Blue Book]. They are excellent sources of information.)

So let's get started. Do not take your car to the detail shop! But pretend you did. Take the $100 plus tax and pay down loans or pay up owns. And then follow these steps:

First, the interior. Empty the car: glove compartment, console, trunk, mats, ashtrays, under the seats, behind the seats, behind the visors…everything must go, except the loose change. Vacuum the car. Vacuum it again. Not one little thread should show. Wash the mats with a brush, water, and a little household detergent. Not too much! Rinse them well. Let them dry.

Gently get rid of stains on the seats, doors, door handles, console, dashboard, and rear deck. Wash the inside of the windows. Use Armor All on the inside leather and vinyl. Wow!

Now the exterior. Wash the car. Wash the wheel wells, the metal parts on the inside of the doors, the door posts, the runners, anywhere you can see dirt. Wash the wheels, tires, and any place that shows dirt. If it is really dirty, wash it again. Wipe it down. Look at it. Miss any spots? Do it again.

Get out the wax. Wax it. Good job. Look for spots you may have missed.

Scour the tires with a brush and Comet. Rinse. Apply Armor All. Good job.

Go see your friend Sam, the auto know-it-all. Ask Sam how to clean an engine with water from a hose. He will tell you to take it to his buddy Peter Profit. Tell him you can't afford it. Sam's know-it-all attitude will take over. He will not only give you instructions, he will do it or supervise you as you do it. He will also check out your car and tell you where you missed a spot or two (don't mind his criticism, he is helping you get more money for your car), or he will tell you how nice your car looks. Tell him, "Thank you." Smile.

Step back. What has the past five hours cost you? Nothing. What has it given you? *A new car.* Almost. But it may not qualify for excellent condition...yet.

How long has it been since you have done the basics: oil change, radiator flush, transmission fluid change, wheel bearings packed, and wiper blades, belts, and hoses replaced? This is what is expected for a car in excellent shape.

Does your car start okay? A prospective buyer might notice if it doesn't. Does it need a tune up? Does your car stop when you brake? A prospective buyer might also notice that. Get a brake job. Tires? Slick is not nice. Excellent condition means that the tires are good. Does the engine make a funny noise? Do not count on the guy having a hearing problem.

Any of these problems should be addressed (read: fixed).

And now you are not foisting a disaster on some poor person who doesn't know a car from an auto. After you sell this car, you will be able to look the Lord and the buyer in the eye. You can tell a prospective customer about the maintenance that you have done. Show the receipts. Top dollar.

On the other hand, look at your car. It is not the disaster you thought it was. After all, you put your special touches on it. It reflects you. In more ways than one.

Tell you what: why don't you just keep it for a little while? It looks good and it runs well. Keep it while you do your research and save for a larger down payment when your research reveals which is the best car for you. The most economical car you can drive, all things considered, is the one in your garage.

BUYING A CAR

At some point you may come to the point of *really* needing to buy a car. Before you rush out to buy that new car smell, I have a few shrewd words of advice for you: The price of today's average new car is $24,000. Cars lose 20 percent of their value the first year or, in this case, a whopping $4,800 or $400 per month. That could buy a lot of gas.

Having said that, I can think of three instances in which someone might want to buy a new car:

1. If you are a salesperson who travels across several states watching the odometer go around and around. Breaking down in January just outside Manhattan, Kansas, is not fun. If your company reimburses at the government-mandated cost per mile, a new car could make sense.

2. If you are an older couple who wants to do more traveling. If other sectors of your financial plan are in order, it might be wise to invest in an automobile that will cause minimal frustration (read: Japanese imports).

3. If you have so much money that you feel good about spending (read: wasting) it.

When was the last time you walked into a new car showroom? The friendly folks there work with you as professionals; you are the amateur. If you don't get real smart real soon, you will be lunch. (But, of course, you will tell your friends what a great deal came your way. Yep, you really put it over on them. You were tough.)

You are becoming a Shrewd Christian interested in building the Net Wealth side of the scale when you know what you are up against. So roll up the mental sleeves; you have work to do.

Doing the Research

First, as a general rule, do not ask friends for advice about purchasing a car. Most of them won't have a clue about the best way to go about it. Roll up your sleeves and do the research yourself.

Second, bring your spouse into the equation. (Only do this if you have a spouse; you do not need to get a spouse before you buy a car.) Do not get all macho and huffy and say, "This is my arena. I know what is best!" After all, your husband may have an idea or two that could be good. Give him the benefit of the doubt.

Third, use the Magic 80 to plan your attack. Get paper, pencil, a calculator, and a cup of coffee. Research is fun, but you do not want to repeat yourself. *Consumer Reports* has an annual auto issue that tells about used cars in detail; it gives the repair histories for every make and model for the last ten years. This issue is the basis for your research. (If you do not own this issue, your library should have it.) It will include recommended cars and nonrecommended cars. It breaks down recommendations into price groupings. Start here, make notes, keep coming back to this issue, and watch how your thoughts change over two weeks of research. Condense your information into one page of a very small notebook. You will take this notebook with you when you venture into the buying jungle. That notebook is your ultimate weapon. It is probably a good idea to keep the complete results of your research in your automobile.

Fourth, decide what is the least amount you are willing to spend on a car. Do you have the money? How long will it take you to get the money? If you need a car but can't afford it, ask yourself *why* you need the car. It had better be job-related, and if it is, put every money-accumulating trick that you learned in this book to work for you to get the money for the car.

Do not even let the evil thought of leasing enter your mind. Leasing is a form of purgatory. It is not quite hell, but you can see it from there. You may ask, "Why? After all, my friends all say that you can drive more car for less money." Let's see, the dealer charges you a hefty down payment and a hefty monthly fee. At the end of the lease period, you must give the car back to him. Would you say you or he won?

Finally, ask yourself what kind of car fits you best? If the big deal is driving to and from work, the grocery store, and church, does a smokin' V-8, 4WD, rompin'-stompin' SUV fit you best? The time to decide this basic stuff is in the privacy of your own residence. As opposed to, for instance, the little room in the back of Dealin' Dan's auto superstore. There, you have way too many auto manufacturers offering way too many styles, models, and trim lines. And we haven't even brought up the issue of color yet. What is the result of too many choices coming at you too fast and too furious? Well, the obvious choice boils down to the auto that had the best ad during the last Super Bowl! Or you could throw a dart.

Before you buy or even get close to buying a car, think seriously about these things:

1. Safety. The National Highway Traffic Safety Administration (www.nhtsa.dot.gov) will put its research at your fingertips for free. You will find out that some companies blare out "Five Star Safety" for one of three tests. They do not tell you what they scored in the other areas. It is up to you to complete the research—in depth! Like a good spousal unit, it is what is underneath that counts. For example, a 2002 Infiniti I30 is a good-looking car with a top-notch reliability rating. You just might want to see how the Infiniti I30 stacks up in safety tests against others in its class. Sorry, Infiniti owners, the news is not good. But I am just relaying the information from the safety testers.

2. Reliability. Consumer Reports is our only defense against disasters. (Reliability is spelled J-a-p-a-n-e-s-e.) Your friendly librarian will help. Or go online and join at www.consumerreports.org.

3. Price. You must know your prices—not only of the car you want but of the options on that car. Two helpful Internet sites—the previously mentioned www.edmunds.com and www.kbb.com (Kelley Blue Book)—will tell you the fair market value of a used car. They will tell you what the car is worth as a trade-in, as a private party purchase, and as a dealer purchase.

4. Cost of ownership. The Web site www.edmunds.com has a little section that will tell you what it will really cost to own a vehicle for five years. Fasten your seatbelt when you get those numbers!

5. Insurability. After you have your selection narrowed down to three to five cars, call your insurance company. Have a list of coverages in front of you. You will find that list on the front page of your auto insurance policy. Ask your current auto insurer how much it would cost to insure the cars you are currently interested in. Now call two or three other companies and ask for the cost of the same insurance for each car. There could be $100 difference between the cost of insurance. Multiply that by five years. Aha!

Making the Purchase

Let's outfox the auto wolves. Let's buy a great used car for much less than the price of a new one. Let's buy an auto that is in good proportion to our Net Wealth. Let's pretend we are millionaires, and do the same thing they do.

If you think about it during a Magic 80 session, you will discover a plethora (many, lots, bunches) of ways to purchase cars that will tip the scale toward Net Wealth. This is why it is so important to know the car price and the option price. Real knowledge leads to the best deal whether from an individual or a dealer. The Web site www.edmunds.com, for instance, can tell you how the mileage of a car affects its price. This is a very nice thing to know, especially when dealing with a private party.

The CMC should know that private-party car buying is divided into two classes: not-friends and friends. Here are some rules for buying a car from not-friends:

1. Hold on to your wallet and be prepared to walk away from any car for *any reason*. You may not even know how to verbalize your thought process; trust your instincts.

2. Do not try to make friends with not-friends; you are buying a car, not enhancing your social life.

3. Be extremely polite. While it is true that you are buying a car, you are also representing the Lord.

4. Know what the private party should be charging for that model of car with options (see www.edmunds.com).

5. Ask to see all the maintenance records. Be wary if the owner does not have the records. Ask where he had the vehicle maintained and if you have his permission to talk with that facility. Call that service. Explain that you are interested in buying this car and may want to continue having the car serviced at that establishment. Ask what has been done and how regularly. (Do not worry. If the car is sold while you are doing your research, remember that there are hundreds more to take its place.)

6. Run a VIN check through www.edmunds.com; no sense in buying a car that was in a wreck, flood, fire, or other natural disaster.

7. Ask questions. Find out where the little sticks are that show fluid levels. (It is a bad sign if the owner of the vehicle does not know how to find those little sticks.) Look at the fluid. Is it low or dirty?

8. Pull out your little book of information. Stare at it for a moment or two. Look the person in the eye. Ask if there is any

room for negotiation in the price. Get a firm, fair bottom-line price. State it back: "Okay, $7,500 is a fair price." But the deal is not done.

9. If you feel that this is the right car, ask to take it to your faithful auto mechanic. The owner should have no problem with that. If he or she balks, walk. It is that simple.

10. If your mechanic says, "Pass on this one," you have just spent the best $100 of your life. If the flaws are normal wear and tear and can be easily fixed, get repair estimates in writing. Put them in your notebook.

11. Revisit the current vehicle owner. Open your little notebook and explain your mechanic's findings. Be very polite. Reduce the asking price by the estimates. (Do not forget to include wiper blades in that reduction.) Tell the owner you believe this is a fair price. Do not waver and do not "split" the cost of the repairs.

12. Be prepared to leave a check for a deposit. In the lower left-hand corner of the check, describe the car, the price, and the deposit.

Now some rules for buying cars from friends:

1. Substitute this question for rule 2 above: "What do you know or suspect is currently wrong with this car in its present condition?" Write down the information. Repeat it back to your friend after you have written it down. Smile.

2. Follow the rest of the rules in the list of rules for buying cars from not-friends.

I bought my last two cars from friends. Good deals, good cars. And we are still friends!

Another good idea: Attend an auto auction with an experienced auto broker. Tell the broker what you want. He or she will give you a professional opinion regarding price range, attend the auction with you, appraise the vehicle, and buy it for you. Auto brokers generally charge a fee. That fee can be a percentage of the cost of the car or a flat fee.

Recently a Colorado Springs auto broker I know bought a four-year-old Acura RL for under $17,000. While such a low price is a very rare occurrence, it shows that good things can happen if you choose to go this route.

While I do not often recommend purchasing a car from a dealer, there are exceptions. Reputable used car and new car dealers (businesses with the same name for five years or more and few or no referrals to the Better Business Bureau) can be a good choice. The cars they have will be the best on the used-car market. In addition, the dealership can be a significant aid in times of trouble.

Let me give you an example. I was giving a seminar to a group of people, and the section on automobiles was the current topic. I went through my little song and dance. A gentleman gave me additional information I had not heard before. He told of buying a preowned Toyota pickup truck (usually one of the most reliable brands) from a dealer. I smiled my best know-it-all smile, thinking he was going to give a disaster story with a sad ending…thus proving my seminar point. However, the joke was on me. The man told of a trip he and his wife took to the East Coast. Thousands of miles away from home, the engine blew up; not fun. The Toyota repair service said $2,500, please. He complained that the truck had been in his possession for less than two weeks. Toyota listened and, *because the Toyota truck had been bought at a Toyota dealership,* they replaced the engine at no cost to the owner. Go figure.

Now a word to the people who are becoming wise: If your current car dies, do not rush out and get transportation by this weekend. If you must have transportation, borrow a family member's car (make sure they have insurance) or rent a car while you do your research. But you may not need a car.

Our '88 Acura died six months ago. (We did not give it a Christian burial.) I wanted to see how long we could wait before we *had* to get a second car. We are still waiting. Seven months. Margie and I must think, communicate, and plan a little more, but we are on the same page. Only one time have we been really frustrated not to have two cars. In the meantime, we are not spending money on the big expenses of a second car. Single-car ownership has its privileges.

You should hear the spirited discussions Margie and I have about what car to buy next. Okay, I lied. Margie does not care what we drive. Well maybe she is developing an opinion. I know she is more vocal than she used to be. Being on the same page allows you to wait until each person has full buy-in. I think I have made the point for a midsize SUV. But don't be surprised if we end up getting a sedan. Who knows? We may reach a decision before I finish this book.

(You want a far-out thought? Let's say you are heavy into the Not Wealth side of the scale; as a matter of fact, you are in danger of moving to the left of Start! It might be in your best interests to go without *any* car for a certain amount of time. If you live within a reasonable distance from services and public transportation, you will be able to get on your financial feet a lot quicker. Remember: CMCers are tough!)

WISE CHOICES

I want to tell you the story of Norm and Molly Guillame. Norm was a public school teacher in Grand Rapids, Michigan, for thirty years. Molly, the only person known to me that could possibly give my wife a run for her money in the "nice" race, was for the most part an RCEO.

Norm: Boring job, fun person. Needs a little external fun. Maybe the car reveals the fun side of Norm. How does a 1992 Oldsmobile 98 sound to you? Not fun?

Listen more closely. Norm retired from teaching at the age of fifty-two. He grabbed a part-time job in his church as the head of discipleship ministries. A job he loves and, not surprisingly, is very good at. Even though he drives a dumpy car.

Did I mention that his kids are fully educated? Or that he lives in a beautiful home in a suburb of Grand Rapids? A home, by the way, that has no mortgage? Or that Norm and Molly are buying a condo on Lake Macatawa in Holland, Michigan?

Norm works part time, remember? So what does he do with the rest of his time? He loves to take his fully paid sailboat out of the Lake Macatawa Bay and onto Lake Michigan. He loves to sail alone—at 2:00 a.m. under a full moon—and enjoy the fruits of a 1992 Oldsmobile 98. He sleeps a little later than you and me. Shoot, he sleeps a *lot* later.

Norm has the secret: Automobiles are for transportation; free time, boats, condos, and great jobs are for fun. You get to have more fun when you buy solid cars that are older.

Cars today can easily last ten to fifteen years. Frugal means that you understand your car does not determine your value. So, yes, we drive an older car. We maintain it well and plan to keep it for another five to seven years. We enjoy what the money we didn't waste on cars enables us to do. The valet at our club gets a great kick out of parking it. He faithfully promises that he will return it in good condition. He never does; he always returns it in the same condition as he took it.

Makes me smile. It's worth it.

STEPS TOWARD SHREWD

- Never use the word *investment* in the same sentence as *automobile*.
- If you are going to sell your current car, take the time to make it look like new.
- Do not buy new cars! Remember that many very rich people own very old cars.
- Do your research before you buy *any* car. Consider safety, reliability, price, cost of ownership, and insurability. Use the Internet (and take notes!) to make the wisest purchase.
- Before you buy a car, ask yourself, Do I want transportation or image? Make the choice that will move you toward the Net Wealth side of the scale.

15

Stuff Happens

Today's world is weird. It was weird before September 11, and it has only gotten weirder since then.

Before then Americans had been insulated from realities (terrorism) that were common in other countries. Now we realize that there is no insurance against terrorists. Their attacks underscore our ultimate vulnerability. Nonetheless, we can limit our vulnerability to more normal events of life. Insurance can become a pillar that protects our families against the ravages of illness and accident.

A friend recently had heart bypass surgery on three blocked arteries. His life was saved by the procedure. The cost of that surgery? $120,000. Now, I don't know about you, but I seldom (okay, never) have $120,000 in my checkbook. That amount of money would chill most people's wealth development program.

It only caused a hiccup in my friend's wealth development program. He had health insurance and had to pay a 10 percent deductible of $12,000. Not a small amount, but he certainly did not have to debate whether to have the surgery or die of a heart attack.

You have heard it said that there are three important things to know about buying a house: "Location, location, location." Because I believe that we must be responsible to our families, I want to tell you three important things you need to know about insurance: "Protection, protection, protection."

Some Christians believe that insurance is a faith buster. We only need to trust God, and He will protect us. Insurance is wasted money. We just need to live in faith to get through tough times. We should not rely on our own efforts. Some people say that if a person is truly in God's will and has a personal, growing relationship with God, he or she should be able to look at any situation without batting an eye. Insurance is an inhibitor of faith.

There is a time to boldly confront situations in faith, and there is a time to be shrewd in dealing with situations. Remember that the apostle Paul, in his early ministry, was being hunted by people who wished to do grievous harm to the traitor who had become a Christian. According to the faith reasoning above, Paul should have stepped out of hiding, confronted his enemies, and allowed God to protect him. What did happen? Why, the apostle Paul scooted out of his enemy's reach by sneaking out of town in a basket let down over the city wall. Where was his faith? Why did he not stand up to the mob?

He understood reality. Trusting God is the right thing to do. But testing God is another thing altogether.

The spiritual types who talk down insurance do not see the reason for insurance—until disaster strikes. For instance, what would happen if instead of buying homeowner's insurance, you used that money to pay off the loan on your home. The day finally arrives when your home is free and clear, and the same day it burns down. The newspaper carrier slips on your stairs and breaks her leg. Your neighbor borrows your truck and causes an accident. I could go on and on. What would we do without the protection insurance offers?

For us today, reality means protecting our families from the consequences of most illnesses, accidents, and disasters. If you only pay money and never use the insurance, it is money well spent. It has afforded you decent sleep. If you pay for insurance and use it, it is money well spent.

Financial wealth for the CMC comes through generosity, a paid-off home, no debt, and a tidy accumulation fund. Insurance is the protector of that wealth.

I can hardly wait for my insurance buddies to call and snort all over themselves that insurance can be a great investment. I am prepared. I will simply ask, "For whom?" They will respond, " 'For whom' what?" I will counter, "For whom is insurance a great investment: for me? Or for you and the insurance company?"

For insurance agents, it is the investment side of the insurance bread that holds the butter, not the protection side. Insurance agents make more money in the same amount of time from whole life or universal policies than from term insurance. They have their tables (impressive). They have their literature (the pictures are really nice). They have their spiel (slick). They have been trained to elicit your objections. They have been trained to destroy your objections with logic, tables, and literature (more nice pictures). They are relentless. They are licensed to kill. I call my agent "008." He calls me cheap. He would call me wonderful if I made his family wealthy at the expense of my family. So know what you want *before* you talk to an insurance company. Otherwise you might get moved by those nice pictures.

As I write this, I am on my deck watching a fight between six crows and a hawk. Apparently, the hawk had ventured into crow territory. But it is not much of a fight. The hawk has settled into the top of a tree and the crows are dive-bombing it. The crows are going nuts. They are screaming and coming at the hawk from all angles. The hawk just looks at them. The crows get close, but not too close. They yell. They threaten. (I don't know if they have any nice pictures.) But the hawk just sits there. The crows grow tired. They are resting on the hill. The hawk is flying away. The crows let him go.

When it comes to dealing with salespeople, be like the hawk: Get what *you* need, not what *they* need. Make sure they sell you what is best for you. Many will not have the best but merely the good. Ignore them. When you buy, buy the best. Make sure the insurance company will be around long enough to make good on the promises they made to you when they took your money.

Doing Your Homework

A basic insurance portfolio could look like this:

1. Health insurance, crucial for any family at any time.
2. Auto insurance, mandated by the state in which you live.
3. Homeowner's insurance if you have a home; renter's insurance if you rent.
4. Life insurance—buy twenty years of term insurance to equal seven years of current salary the minute you and your spouse begin to work on having a family. When you have a solid Net Wealth, let this insurance drop.
5. Disability insurance—often overlooked, but in my opinion the chances of being disabled for a period of time are greater than the chances of accidental death. When you have a solid Net Wealth, think about letting this drop.
6. Umbrella insurance to protect against what your auto and homeowner's insurance do not cover.
7. Long-term care insurance.

Okay, you have decided to protect, protect, protect. Now it is time to also shop, shop, shop.

How long have you been with your auto, home, and life insurance companies? If you said three years or longer, you could be cramming money into the trash compactor. Gather your insurance papers. Don't know where they are currently living in your home? Search until you find them. I will wait.

Good. Now mark a file folder and put it in your file cabinet/drawer/ place. It has a home! Be proud! Look at the coverage page. If your eyes glaze over, take a deep breath, do two pushups and remind yourself you are getting your SC (Shrewd Christian) degree. Do you need to increase or decrease coverage? For example, if your home cost $150,000, you need not insure it for that whole amount. A disaster will destroy the house but should leave the land and the foundation intact. Make adjustments. I would suggest you have inflation and replacement cost riders in your policy.

Now get the phone book. You are about to enter Fun Land!

Start calling the big boys. Tell them what you are doing. Would they like to bid for your business? Does Tiger Woods like golf? If you don't understand something, ask a question. Whenever I reach a place of confusion (which is quite often), I will stop a salesperson and say, "Did you know this is national stupid question month? And I have one."

People always chortle and come back in very patronizing tones, "Oh, there is no such thing as a stupid question. How can I help you?" And they answer my question. Only occasionally do I have two or three people break into hysterical laughter and shout to their workmates, "Wait until you hear this geek's question." I usually hang up and make a mental note to not call that company again.

Savings? Homeowner's insurance with our current company is $962. With a new company: $746 for more coverage. And by the way, this company also insures cars. Auto insurance with our current company: $1,210. With the new company, including a discount for getting home and auto together: $630. Total savings: $796. Total time: one hour and forty-two minutes. Not bad.

It gets better. You have $796 of real money that could be used for play, debt reduction, or padding your accumulation fund. If you have credit-card debt, that $796 would help defray some expensive interest charges. So instead of making a minimum payment, include an extra $796 on your next bill. Let's see, $796 at a 19.21 percent interest rate is $153 in savings.

Auto Insurance

The most important factoid about auto insurance is this: Learn to drive. Seriously. No more tickets. Not even a parking ticket. They cost money:

The cost of the ticket and the jump in the price of your insurance damage the Net Wealth side of your scale. No more accidents. They cost money: the cost of repairs and the jump in the price of your insurance do the same damage.

Let me be firm with you: No more tickets! Never, never, and never!

Recently a friend and I were reviewing the potential savings involved in auto insurance. As usual I was giving my upbeat approach. The more info I gave him, the glummer his facial expression. He finally spoke up and mentioned that he and his wife had a "few" tickets and three accidents in the last three years. They were in a "high-risk" (read: expensive) auto-insurance bracket. Approximately 40 percent more than sane drivers. End of potential savings. However, in three years their record could be clean. I was gentle but firm as I told him how poor driving hurt his Net Wealth.

Never get a ticket!

Did I tell you I recently met Officer Bigelow of the Wyoming State Police?

He will tell you that the above words are very, very true. I had a nice conversation with Officer Bigelow about this matter. He was obviously a people person because he asked me questions about myself as we got to know each other. He said, "Do you know what the speed limit is? Do you know how fast you were going? Do you know that you were driving sixteen miles over the speed limit?" I had only one correct answer out of three.

But I played my aces: "Sir, I am returning from Seattle. My father-in-law just passed away."

"Mr. Atkinson, I am sorry to hear that."

"Today is my thirty-fourth wedding anniversary, and I am hurrying home to Margie."

"Mr. Atkinson, congratulations on thirty-four years...not many people get to that number these days. But sir, what does this information have to do with your exceeding the speed limit?"

I was out of aces and out $88—and whatever my insurance company will do to me when their computers learn about my citation. I guess I could try to make the case that I received a citation instead of a ticket. But like Officer Bigelow, you wouldn't buy that ace.

Use the same principles to protect your wealth that you used to get your wealth: Pay attention, compare prices, and above all, invest in the well-being of your relationships.

STEPS TOWARD SHREWD

- The purpose of insurance is protection. Insurance is not an investment.
- Whether or not you have to use your insurance, it is money well spent. Not having insurance is not shrewd!
- Research insurance before you buy. Buy only what *you* believe you need, not what the sales machines say you need.
- No more tickets! Officer Bigelow agrees.

16

Caution: Investing Can Be Dangerous to Your Wealth!

Can you explain the difference between gambling, and investing? Listen up, because it is tricky.

When you lose at gambling, it is bad because it is sin and therefore not honorable. When you lose in the stock market, it is good because you invested, and it is very honorable.

Get it? Of course, both situations resulted in losses. But which ones can you safely talk about during fellowship hour after church?

Okay, time for further elucidation (that means, essentially, clarification...my editor likes me to use an occasional big word to prove I am "learned"). Consider the following dictionary definitions:

1. "To put money into a business, stocks, bonds, or real estate for the purpose of obtaining income or making a profit."
2. "An act or undertaking involving risk of a loss."

There you have it, clear and simple. The two definitions listed are for the words *invest* and *gamble*. Notice the positive spin on the first, and the negative spin on the second. The definitions are incomplete. To the first we should add, "but a loss is a distinct possibility." To the second, we should add, "but a gain is a distinct possibility."

Everyone knows that gambling is wrong but investing is honorable. Gambling sends people to poverty. Investing sends people to wealth.

Well, in the words of an auto-rental commercial: "Not exactly!"

I am not suggesting that everyone should migrate to Las Vegas. I am suggesting that for many (if not most) CMCers, investing in stocks, bonds, or a business is a gamble. You do not know whether you will win or lose. Professionals in the world of finance spend every day of their lives on this stuff. (I can only imagine doing that if I were assigned to the place other than heaven.) You spend a few spare moments on that stuff. Remember the sheep and the wolves thing? Time for shrewd.

Gambling and investing are alike in that they both contain an element of *risk*. You can win at stocks, bonds, and real estate as well as blackjack, the slots, and the Wheel of Fortune. You can also lose. The more you stand to gain, the larger the risk. Therefore, the more you also stand to lose.

A Dangerous Choice

You know those little warning signs on every pack of cigarettes? "Warning: Smoking could be hazardous to your health." I think each stock transaction should have a similar warning. In bold print.

"WARNING: Investing could be hazardous to your wealth!"

Instead, the sanitized warning of the investment community reads as follows: "While there is no guarantee that future returns will match previous performance…" and quickly moves on to tell you of the wonderful gains you will make.

If you do not have a talent or stomach for risking your hard-earned money, if you do not have the interest or the time to become a savvy investor, if you cannot afford financial planners, congratulations, you are in the middle class.

There is a fallacy in the thinking of investment gurus. They like to flaunt: "Historically, the stock market has outperformed any other investments by averaging a 10.63 percent annual gain, *including* during the Great Depression years! Therefore, the stock market is the place for your money." The trick is getting your money out of the market at the right time. Did you know that between 1965 and 1981, the market went down 10 percent?

We have gone over this before. But it is important. I should have understood it in my earlier life. Several times in my earlier life. How much of that 10 percent return was due to dividends? More than 4 percent! Are companies paying dividends today? Stop laughing. Fiscal sleight of hand is a nasty thing.

If I had written this in 1999, people would be throwing this book in the trash pile. Everyone was headed toward wealth; a 20 percent annual return in the market was expected. And it would go on forever. In April of 2000, a stockbroker friend of ours put together a plan for my family to invest our first $100,000 in a zero-coupon government bond. The rest of the amount we wanted to invest would go into his favorite mutual fund. (The one that paid him a large commission so he could wear new suits and have an office on an upper floor with a view of the Rockies.) The market was at 11,400 points, and books were coming out with titles like *Dow at 30,000*. Wow!

We didn't do his deal. He was not happy. Told me to call him when we got some nerve. He slammed the phone down. Literally. We had taken away his commission, and we were *chickens*. Ha! This morning (three years later) the market was at 8,442. A drop of approximately 3,000 points or 26 percent. Ouch.

I am tempted to call him today and ask him, "Okay, let's pretend we had invested with you. We now have lost a lot of money. What rate of return must we get over how many years to equal what we started with in 2000?" Nah, I decided not to call him. I hate having the phone slammed. Hurts my ears. We chickens are like that.

I read an article on a mutual fund's Web site: "The biggest risk is not taking one!" It was written to us. They are trying to tell us that safety is risky and if we don't invest with them, we will be raped and pillaged by inflation. I'm not convinced; I believe those things that could hurt us and may escalate in price (e.g., medical costs) can be managed through insurance.

I would urge you to replace the CPI (consumer price index) with the YPPI (Your Personal Price Index, pronounced, "YIPPEEE!"). Inflation does not hold true for everything. It is said that inflation of such and such a rate over thirty years will reduce the value of your dollar to a pittance. Everything will always go up, and nothing will ever come down. If that were true and we use 1974 as our base, we should have gas prices at $5 per gallon, chicken should cost $3 per pound, and *nothing* should cost less than it did thirty years ago. Last week gas was $1.49 per gallon, chicken was 49¢ per pound, and a lot of things cost less today than they did in 1974. If we tried to compute current prices back to 1970's prices, it would mean they are giving food to us!

Remember the calculator you paid $70 for in 1973? You can buy a better one today for $7. The fax machine that cost you $1,800 in 1983 costs $200 today. The refrigerator you purchased for $900 in 1985 costs $650 today. The big deal on investing is that you never know where the market will be when you need the money. Think of all the people who were planning a nice cozy retirement starting in 2000 or 2001 or 2002 or 2003. Surprise! Think Enron.

BECOME YOUR OWN FINANCIAL ADVISOR

What is a stockbroker? It is important that we take the sheep's clothing off such persons to reveal what is underneath their expensive clothing and automobiles. Please understand this important investment advice: Stock-brokers are stock sellers: sales machines. They only make money when you buy and sell stock. That is the only way they can feed their families. You are the means to that end. Period.

I know, I know. They will tell you that they are not successful unless you are successful; every good stockbroker has their clients' best interests at heart. Blah, blah, and a resounding BLAH!

My research revealed this tidbit from the *Wall Street Journal,* March 14, 1991: "Financial Planners Squabble Over Creating Code of Conduct." Some of the questions planners were debating at the time:

- Should planners be required to place clients' interests ahead of their own in all circumstances? Duh!
- Should planners be required to solve clients' problems through "appropriate financial procedures," such as suggesting they pay off debt before suggesting financial products? Double duh!
- Should planners be required to disclose how much compensation they will receive if clients buy products they recommend? Good grief!

Are those questions debatable? Not to me, and certainly not to you.

The next time you are talking finances, investing, leasing, and buying, and someone is helping you see the world from his or her perspective, ask yourself this question: Is this person looking out for his or her kids or for my kids? The answer should be both; often it is not.

In addition, financial advisors are almost always wrong for you because they do not know you, and you do not know them. Oh, they can take detailed surveys and run a computer-driven interview, but they do not know you. They will only give token acknowledgment to the centrality of your walk with Christ. They will urge you to invest with them rather than invest with the Lord. They are wrong about you from the get-go because they assume that the base of your life is economic. They assume, therefore, that you are essentially an *economic* person. They deal with your finances as the most basic but *separate* entity of your lives. And you let them because you do not know where to begin, and life is too short for understanding the investment thing.

But you say with a little glow of excitement in your eye, "My broker/advisor is a Christian! And a fine one at that. Why, he (or she) is a leader in our church! What do you say to that?"

I say this: You can possibly trust him or her, but do your homework; know what you are doing. Did I mention that my friend the stockbroker in the above illustration was also in a weekly Bible study with me? Do a few pilot projects with the broker to test the waters. I should have done that. Do you win after fees, commissions, and other expenses are deducted? Investment expenses *lower* your real rate of return.

It is true that millionaires spend an inordinate amount of time with financial advisors. It is also true that they have an inordinate amount of money. It is true that we can spend an inordinate amount of time with tax advisors. It is also true that we do *not* have an inordinate amount of money. CMC advisors, therefore, will be found on the shelves of our local library. Your accumulation/investing goal over the next three years: Become your own financial advisor.

Stay away from magazines that tell you how to get rich this week. Two reasons:

1. Eighty percent of the advertising is from stocks and bonds people. (Ask yourself, Why would financial institutions advertise in money magazines? If you think they would answer, "Because money magazines toe the party line and can help get me clients who can pay my children's way through college," then you get it.)
2. After they have said, "You should live on less than you earn," they have nothing to say the next month, so they dig up other things to say every thirty days.

The Shrewd Christian Invests

Allow me to quote, uncensored, from an e-mail sent to me by my editor: "In the investment section, a reader might wonder, *So, how did Neil get wealthy? Was there one big investment that paid off, does he have a secret investment strategy, or was it really all these little things?*"

Yes, besides doing a lot of Little Things Excellently over Time and Applying them Appropriately, there is a little-known, essentially secret investment strategy I discovered and have been using for a long time. This strategy is disappointed with gains of a mere 10 percent and gets giddy with regular returns of 60 to 150 percent!

One has to be a little disciplined, do a little homework, develop a knack for timing, and then act! This strategy is so safe that your only anxiety will be that the results are too good to be true. But the gains will be so stupendous that you will be wondering why you haven't heard this strategy trumpeted in every publication in the country.

The reason that it is not well known and publicized is that it is not sexy.

First of all, you must come up with $1,000. No, you may not borrow it. No, not even from Aunt Betty. No borrowing. You might have to sell a few worthless things, eat lentils, eat at home, brown-bag at work, but you can get the money.

Okay, you have the money? Good. Here is the investment strategy of increasing the asset side of your ledger. A major financial goal for Margie and I was to increase our assets. Let me show you how, with absolutely no risk, you can get a huge return on investment this month.

Make your monthly mortgage payment. At the same time, pay an additional $1,000 to principal. You have now increased your Net Wealth base by $1,000.

Excuse me, that illustration is not a dirty trick, and yes, we did go over that in chapter 13. I know you thought I could not have become wealthy on little things alone, and I know that when you heard I had a secret investment strategy, your little heart went pitter-patter. And even faster when I said, "a little-known, essentially secret investment strategy." You knew there had to be something I was holding back. And you finally thought I was going to come clean and fess up. Nonetheless, in your haste to grab the "secret," you let the lesson from the earlier chapter slip out of your brain. In the future, guard your brain.

You need to be reminded that investing *should* increase your asset base. It *should* guarantee huge returns, and then live up to that guarantee.

But *accumulation* is much more important than investing. Will Rogers once said that he was more concerned about the return *of* his investment than about the return *on* his investment. Your concern should be about developing a reservoir of money. Accumulating resources is paramount; investing comes later. You will want to recognize that after you have read enough, you will be very careful with your nest egg, your accumulation fund. It took a while to make that fund appear; it will take a nanosecond to make it disappear.

Once again, no matter what your *stated* rate of return is, you must figure in your investment costs to arrive at your *real* rate of return.

A major illustration: You purchase $1,000 worth of stock, and in one year that stock grows by 10 percent (nice!) and your stockseller/broker says, "Let's take some profits off the table; let's sell." How much do you have? $1,100? No. Silly you. You have $1,100 minus commissions ($50 in and $50 out) or $1,000. But there is an emotional payoff: You can tell the Bible study that you made 10 percent on Shamu Industries.

A minor illustration: Paper towels at one grocery store averaged $1.25 per roll; at another, paper towels averaged 41¢ on sale. A return on investment of 84¢. I bought fifty rolls (essentially a year's supply). My investment netted me $42. If I am in debt, I reinvest that $42 into my credit-card account, and my investment lowers my Not Wealth and therefore raises my Net Wealth. If I am free and clear, I can add it to my accumulation fund. Or I smirk when Margie says, "Let's go out to dinner." My Net Wealth is glowing. (By the way, you do cut your paper towels in half, don't you? They last 50 percent longer that way.)

The CMC should be much more concerned about accumulation than investing. Building a nest egg is much more intelligent than relying on investing to magically transport you to the land of the rich and famous. You will have to fight to build a nest egg. Then you will, like a mother bird, have to fight like crazy to keep the nest egg from those who want a piece of it.

Your hard-won nest egg will get to maturity when you:

1. maximize life;
2. live frugally but not cheaply;
3. let a little grow into a lot; and
4. look for value, not growth. (Value investments mean they have value. Growth investments mean that someday they may have value.)

The ABCs of Investing: Always Be Conservative

In my opinion, ABC is the right way for normal middle-class people, unless you are willing to and like to put an inordinate amount of time into investing. Many unscrupulous investment counselors (Christians among them) are ready to apply the shears to sheep like you and me. We can get fleeced in a moment, and then we are standing buck naked in the cold. And the shearers don't care. They are out looking for another little lamb. Since they only fleeced and didn't kill you, their conscience is clear.

Let's say you are thirty-five years old and have a small amount of money in your retirement account. You have been burned by other people's advice. You have also been burned by your own silly mistakes. You are paralyzed by your experiences. What to do?

First, recognize that you will likely live another forty-five years.

Second, set a goal that you will use the first 10 percent of that time (4.5 years) to become a reasonably decent investor. Nothing good happens fast. In the meantime, do not let any of your retirement dollars get lost. You will need them when you retire.

Safety of principal is the core of your investment program. Refuse to take chances. Refuse to lose. Keep what you gained, add to it, and let the return be decent. Do not take risks. Protect yourself from increased medical costs by buying proper insurance.

"But Neil, my broker said I should be more aggressive in my early adult years. She said that even if I make mistakes, time will help me out." Exactly. You *will* make mistakes because the greater the chance for profit, the more risk and the greater chance for failure. What happens if you determine *never* to lose money?

"But Neil, my broker convinced me that the biggest risk was not to take a risk. She pointed out that only those who risk big, win big. I want to be BIG. Therefore, safety of principal is risky!"

Well, Bucky, first thing you do is get rid of that broker-salesperson. She has sold you, a solid middle-class Christian, a load of fairy tales. Repeat after me: The tooth fairy is dead. As dead as the argument that safety is risky.

Accumulation with teensy-weensy risk is crucial. (Minimal risk is too risky.) Major in accumulation, not in investing. There is little or no risk involved in accumulation. Earning 27 percent on $1,000 is nice, but the risk to principal is enhanced. Earning 5 percent on $100,000 is nicer because the risk to principal is reduced.

Make compound interest work for you. Believe in Einstein. Get a compound interest chart. Look at it when you are leaning toward greed.

As we've already discussed, compound interest can work for you or against you. When compound interest is working *for* you, it looks like a mountain. It cannot fall on you and hurt you because it is stable. This mountain is about nest egg and accumulation. When compound interest is working *against* you, the mountain is inverted—the top is pointing down. It can easily fall over on you and crush you. This mountain is about debt.

We are after Net Wealth. Wealth is assets, what you own; the larger your asset base, the greater your Net Wealth. To develop wealth, we are after solid, guaranteed gains. There is no such thing as a bad profit. The quick hit can turn into the quick miss. When you gazed lovingly at your pension in 1999, you were thinking of early retirement. Today, as you gaze dumbfounded at your pension, you are thinking of never retiring. On the other hand, the home in which you live has quietly, steadily, and honorably increased your asset base (read: your wealth).

Here is the strategy: Get rid of D1 and D2 debt. Major in D3 debt. Free yourself from "owing." A quick reminder: D1 is Devastating Debt (i.e., owing money for things that are depreciating in value); D2 is Decent Debt (i.e., owing money for things that are appreciating in value); and D3 is Delightful Debt (i.e., other people or companies that owe you money).

Here is a four-step program to phenomenal financial wealth—in other words, a plan for wealth that does not include investing:

1. Pay off your house.
2. Use the former mortgage payment to pay for your kids' education.
3. Use the former mortgage payment/educational funds to add to your retirement reservoir.
4. Smile. A lot.

IF YOU "MUST" INVEST IN THE STOCK MARKET

If you are not a smart investor and you will not take the time to become one, please invest in mutual funds or U.S. Treasuries. But let's say you have worked diligently at accumulating your nest egg. Now how can you maximize it?

The first thing we talked about with regard to buying a car was safety. The first thing we need to talk about in our investment chapter—good job, you are way ahead of me! Of course, it is safety (a.k.a. "teensy-weensy risk").

Big boy and big girl investors (read: rich) divide their investment money into two groups: retirement and gambling (they will use the sophisticated word *speculation,* but that word means gambling).

We, the CMC, will not divide our investment money. We will put all of it into funding a home and education (before age forty), as well as our retirement. We will not be tempted by greed to "gamble or speculate" until we become rich (read: "It will never happen.").

A business cannot exist if it allows the costs of business to get out of control. That business will go down in flames with a loud popping noise as it hits the earth. The CMC will not exist if it allows the costs of investing to get out of control. (Picture flames and a loud popping noise.) The costs of investing are critical to long-term success. For instance, if you use a broker, there will be commissions and fees. If you go to a mutual fund, there could be a front-end charge, marketing expenses (yes, they will charge you for selling their product to you and to others), fees, and management costs.

That is, unless you go to Vanguard. In 1975, Vanguard was founded with the idea of looking after its investors—no front-end charges, no marketing charges, few fees and teensy-weensy management expenses. Therefore, your real rate of return on your investment is higher. Go to their Web site, www.vanguard.com. Locate their tool comparing Vanguard expenses to any other mutual fund company in our country. Choose a comparable fund from Vanguard and the other company. Follow directions and enter the amount of investment, the number of years the investment will be held, and the expected rate of return. Push the Enter button.

Look at the staggering amount you could have spent in expenses at the other company. Look at the staggering amount you could have saved in expenses at Vanguard. I did this little exercise yesterday. In my hypothetical case, I plugged in the numbers, and in five short years, Vanguard gave me an extra $6,000 compared to the other company. What would I have had to do to earn that $6,000 at Vanguard? Nothing. What would I have had to do at the other company? Work at my job…a lot longer.

The nutshell: (1) become knowledgeable; (2) it is important to be safe; (3) let compound interest work for you; and (4) have patience.

There, is that brain surgery? No, it isn't even hangnail surgery.

WHAT'S HOT, WHAT'S NOT

What does *Money* magazine say this month? What did it say last month? What excuse, analysis, or hypothesis did your stockbroker give you yesterday? What did he or she say today about the next potential Microsoft?

What does Uncle Alfred have to report? (You might just watch CNN as that is where he gets his tidbits. But he feels important by dispensing financial gems as if they were his own, and that is good at his age.)

Where do we get our money information? How do we use that information? How do we build Net Wealth? How can we come from behind, go neck and neck but win the financial race? Or better yet, how can we take the lead at the start of the race and lead all the way to the finish line?

Everyone is looking for the "edge," the one little-known secret that will pole-vault over the rest of the suckers who do not have the edge. The Holy Grail exists, and it is the same one that sent Ponce de Leon to Florida in search of the Fountain of Youth, the forty-niners to the gold fields, and the sooners to the land rush of opportunity. True, a few made it. A lot more lost it. Most arrived too late.

The same is true today. Only the name of this year's grail is the NYSE or NASDAQ. A few make it. A lot more lose it. Most of us arrive too late. Just hold on; over the long haul nothing beats stocks. Blah, blah, blah, and one final BLAH!

I want something that works. It has to be simple so that even my feeble brain can adjust to it. It has to be so safe that the odds of ever losing one penny are slim to none. It has to be backed by the best guarantee known to humankind.

My Aunt Nell had a great recipe for poached pheasant. Her secret was in gathering the ingredients for the meal. Her notes said, "First, get the pheasant." She delighted in saying that you can't have poached pheasant without a pheasant. Amazing that some people would begin to cook without the main ingredient.

It is just as amazing that some people will only accumulate a small amount and count on big returns to create wealth. Accumulation is more important than investing. Little Things done Excellently over Time will give you the steady (and continuing) accumulation to become financially wealthy.

STEPS TOWARD SHREWD

- The only difference between investing in the stock market and gambling is that you can talk about investing at a church coffee hour.
- Accumulation is more important than investing.
- If you must invest, be conservative.
- Start to gain knowledge, but aim to never lose a dollar.
- Enjoy positive compound interest and be patient.
- Don't buy into the lie that investing is the only way to be wealthy.

17

Help the IRS Build Your Wealth

Without taxes we would not have many of the things we take for granted, such as highways, the military, parks, emergency services, and libraries. But taxes intimidate most normal people. They shouldn't. Normal people can do taxes…and profit from the experience.

Many Christians are not good stewards in the area of taxes; we over-withhold. Many will say they would like to be more generous to the Lord but simply do not have the means. Yet they look forward to that tax refund. It comes in mighty handy to pay off bills they have rung up.

Good news: If you pay the Lord first, your charitable giving deduction will go up, and it may bring you over the top to where you can itemize on Schedule A instead of taking the standard deduction. That means you can fill out a new W4 and reduce the amount of money upon which you pay taxes. Therefore, you have legitimately become more of a Shrewd Christian. Not only is it legal and honest, it is the right thing to do.

So how do we use taxes to gain wealth? First, it is *not* shrewd to short-change the government. To have the benefits our country provides, we need to pay our fair share of this financial burden. But not more than our fair share.

Former Supreme Court Justice Learned Hand once said, "You must pay the government every penny that you owe, but you *are not required to pay one penny more than you owe*" (emphasis added). By the way, his name is not a joke—it is a great name for a judge. The name alone should have qualified him. If it is good enough for the Supreme Court of our country, it is good enough for me. Let the federal government help you build your wealth. They will not do it willingly, nor are they stopping you from doing it. In this case, a little tax knowledge gained year by year will go a long way to help your Net Wealth.

We can force the federal government to give us money. We will not do it illegally nor in any way compromise our Christian standards. The government will help us merely because we have information that frees us to act in our own best interests.

No, I am not anti-American, but there is nothing patriotic about unintentionally overpaying our taxes. There is something...I don't know, the word *dumb* comes to mind...about it. I mean, it is one thing to give money rent-free to the government and get it back (that is what you do if you get a refund). It is entirely another matter to give money to the government and let them keep it (that is what you do when you do not know and take advantage of personal tax savings). Government is not known for frugality. If you feel that the way to be patriotic is to pay more taxes, fine. But do it intentionally, not blindly.

No Fear

My daughter called recently with a tax question. I answered the best I could.

She said, "Well, I just never want to face an audit with the IRS."

I asked, "Why not?"

"Everyone says they are horrible."

"In what way are they horrible?"

"Dad, are you always going to act like a dad?"

"Yes."

"To tell the truth, I don't know why audits are horrible, I just heard it. I think it has something to do with records that I may not have."

"Jodi, do you have your pay stubs and your W2?"

"Yes."

"You are fine. Those documents are all you will need for an audit since you don't need to itemize. The IRS policy book was thought up in mental hospitals. But it is implemented by humans beings. Some are ogres, some nice, and some in between. The only thing that should cause nervousness is if you cheat."

"I would never think of cheating."

"I know. But dads have to say those things. That is the only way they can get a bad rap. Moms can say all the nice things. That is the only way they get a good rap. Moms are too smart to do taxes."

Where did Jodi get the idea that an audit of her taxes was something to be avoided at all costs? I don't know. But knowledge is power.

I was audited twice by the IRS. The first time I was nervous and I don't know why; I had not knowingly cut any corners. The agent began the session with: "Mr. Atkinson, is there anything you would like to tell me about this return, or would you like to file an amended return?"

I was puzzled the first time but answered truthfully: "No, why do you ask?"

"Mr. Atkinson, you give too much money away for a person of your income. What do you live on?" I explained our lifestyle. He then took me through the audit and discovered that I owed the government $48. Wow!

The very next year I was audited again. I mean, if they catch a big-time tax evader, let's get him again and again. This time I was not nervous; I was eager and thought I was fully prepared. It turns out I wasn't as prepared as I thought.

The audit began with the same question asked by the first agent. I was not puzzled by it and still answered truthfully, "No, I do not want to declare any more income or file an amended return. That return is true based on my understanding of proper procedures. I made a mistake last year, but I am confident that this year there are no mistakes."

"You give away too much money. What do you live on?"

I again explained our lifestyle. He stared at me for thirty seconds. It seemed like five years. Then he said, "Let's go over your return." He asked for several documents, shook his head, pounded on his calculator. It turns out I had, again, made a mistake. "I am sorry Mr. Atkinson, you missed a few deductions. The government owes you $63. Your check will be in the mail. Thank you for coming in."

I have never again been audited.

You might say, "If you had used a professional, you wouldn't have made those mistakes." Three reasons why I am glad that I did not use a tax professional: (1) even tax professionals make mistakes; (2) if I used a tax professional, I would always be dependent on someone else for something that, for most CMCers, is easy to do; and (3) I would have to pay the preparer a fee.

However, if your return is complicated for whatever reason (inheritance, starting a new business, major illnesses, death, divorce, etc.), get professional advice. My CPA, Marc Boyce, was worth his weight in gold as I started out my business. We became friends. This year he called to remind me that I needed to get my tax information to him as we were running out of time. I casually mentioned that my taxes were already filed and that I had done the work. I will never forget his response, "Your *corporate* returns?" "Yes." I then mentioned that I needed to be authentic for this book. He wasn't too sure about it. I am. Not to worry, I will be seeing Marc next week about other financial matters.

Timing

Most tax professionals understand most of the tax code, but even for the pros, there are fuzzy gray areas open to interpretation. Those fuzzy areas apply to people with complicated returns (people who have a lot of money or a business and are attempting to minimize taxes). Rich people spend a lot of time with their tax advisors. They should. But we are the CMC. We are not rich. We do not need to spend a lot of time with tax advisors; we *do* need to spend some time learning how to properly handle how the tax code applies to our particular situation.

Remember: Normal people can do taxes. You do not have to pay a CPA $100 to fill out the short form. You can take that money and pay down your debt or add to your accumulation fund. Either way, you have increased your Net Wealth and decreased your Not Wealth.

Okay, here is more good news. You (preferably with your spouse) can start on taxes in November, not April. I am suggesting you do your taxes for the year in November before they are due in April.

You are now thinking, "This guy is not making sense. I always did my term papers the night before. Now he wants me to do my taxes four months in advance. I want to postpone pain, not live with it longer than necessary."

If those thoughts went through your brain, let me ask a few questions:
- What grade did you get on those term papers?
- Was your teacher a fraud or did he or she make you work?
- Did you get a financial reward for your term papers?

The answers to the first two questions usually indicate the result of poor time management (e.g., poor grades—unless your teacher was a fraud and handed out high grades because he or she liked you).

The answer to the third question is relevant to your current situation. You will get a knowledge reward for your research that will lead to a financial reward. Using the Magic 80 in November will make April a breeze. Unless you are receiving a refund, in which case you will file in early February. (And promise never to make that mistake again!) That means you will get your refund about the time your friends are starting in on their taxing labors.

Butting heads with the IRS in the knowledge game takes work and time—or in the language of the Shrewd Christian, toughness. The result is fascinating. You invest a few hours in November, and as you put the forms and facts together, you will see ways to save tax dollars (read: lower your taxes). You invest a few hours in November and gain confidence for April—*every April for the rest of your life.*

You will also discover strategies that will keep you above water.

One November as I was going through my annual tax routine, I discovered that we had not paid our tithe, not even close. It had been a wild year with a number of deaths as well as the normal expected and unexpected expenses. But this was the first time in our marriage we had failed to give at least 10 percent of our income to the Lord. I was saddened and embarrassed but thought, "Well, we will just have to do better next year." At that moment I heard a Small Cough. I knew the Source of that Cough. I tried to argue, but the point of the Cough was valid. If I let down this year, it would be easy to let down next year. I borrowed the money and paid the church and the missions that were counting on us. I also vowed to never hear that Cough again.

Let's say you are forty years old. You sweat bullets to understand the tax code *as it applies to you and your situation.* You do not have to memorize the whole thing, just know how to make it play fair as far as you and your family are concerned. We want a level playing field. No, actually we want the playing field tilted in our favor. Knowledge does that. Stuart Kessler, a New York CPA, has indicated that those who get organized earlier pay less in taxes—their organization of records, receipts, and so forth pays off in found deductions.[1] I assume you want the payoff of those "found deductions." Let's go looking.

TACKLING THE FORMS

November. You dedicate your Magic 80 to taxes. No dillydallying. Get the file folder that holds the information on taxes from last year, including the instruction book. Decide to understand all the tax forms. Once you understand them, you will wish you had started this plan years ago. It is not too late. (It is true the forms are complex. A fourth-grader would have trouble with them, but a sixth-grader should be able to master them in an hour or so.)

These forms, when deciphered, pour money into the proper side of the Not Wealth/Net Wealth Scale. They tell you: (1) how to reduce your taxes; (2) how to stop the IRS from using your money without paying interest to you; and (3) how a few hours of reading, researching, and taking action can account for more dollars delivered to your door.

There is a cost. You have to invade the mind of the IRS. That is ominous. They make it so. But it's worth it.

The W4

Did you have to pay federal taxes last year? You did? How much? Not much? Good! You are doing fine. The idea is to give the government the monthly amount they say is due them, but no more. They will not give you interest on your overpayment, they will just refund it. On the other hand, if you do not withhold enough during the year, they will want their money PLUS interest PLUS, possibly, a penalty. Seems a little one-sided, doesn't it?

Okay, let's say you not only didn't have to pay taxes in April of last year but you received a refund of $1,800. You mention that the money came in handy to pay for some of the things you bought at Christmas. Time to start being tax shrewd.

The immediate exercise is to fill out a new W4. Where do you get one? Try your payroll department or your boss. They may fuss a little. That is okay. Their frowns are the price you pay for a raise given by the government. Thank them for the trouble. (You are going to need them again next month.)

The W4 has the complexity of a brick. It is so simple to understand that you will only need twenty of your Magic 80 minutes to understand it, and one minute to fill it out. If you received a refund and you expect you will be at the same place next year, raise the number of exemptions. Line C. You get one for yourself, one for your spouse, and one for each of your kids, and more for the total amount on Schedule A (itemized deductions). Line C is the one you use to raise your exemptions because of your items listed in Schedule A of the 1040. Do not go to sleep on me. We are talking serious money here! Raise the number of exemptions to the point where you are giving the government their pound of flesh, but do not allow them to have any blood or bone.

Because you will not get a refund of $1,800 next year, you just gave yourself a raise of, for the sake of simplicity, $150 per month for twenty-one minutes worth of work. What does that average out to on an hourly basis? You will pay the exact amount of taxes that you owe. You will owe nothing and receive nothing. You will use that extra $150 to be generous to the Lord, pay down debt, or add to your accumulation fund. But you are not through yet. You have more savings ahead.

By using the other fifty-nine minutes of one week's Magic 80, you gain confidence in your ability to do taxes. You fire your tax-preparation expert. You have saved $100. You also find that by adjusting your end-of-year giving (making more contributions in December, perhaps paying January's portion of tithe in late December rather than on January 1), you will save money.

Now make your January mortgage payment on December 31. You can add the interest for that month to this year's taxes on Schedule A under "Interest."

Firing the tax expert	$100 (after-tax money)
Charitable contribution	$ 37
Mortgage deduction	<u>$150</u>
Total:	$287

That's $287 for a few minutes work! Best of all, it is tax free (literally!).

Our success formula will go into a feeding frenzy if you apply that $287 toward your desired result: either downing the Not Wealth side of the scale or upping the Net Wealth side of the scale.

1040

Look at the 1040 form. Did you take a standard deduction or itemize your deductions? If you took a standard deduction, did you take it out of habit or because you worked it both ways? Because the standard deduction was raised in 2003, it would be wise to look closely at what would work best for your situation.

Many people take the standard deduction on the 1040EZ. It is easy. But easy is not tough and it is not shrewd. Taking the easy way means you end up with less money.

Schedule A

Look at Schedule A. It is not scary. Look at it. Good. This is a form. It is easy to understand, and it can help you stop throwing money away.

Many people do not fill out Schedule A. They think it is too much trouble. The IRS estimates that a million Americans could get more money back if they would take the time to fill out Schedule A. How much money? On average $100 per person. That is the IRS talking. You should listen to them. It is expensive to be naive.

This form asks simple questions:

1. Did you have medical expenses totaling over 7.5 percent of line 31 (your adjusted gross income)? If so, how much more? Add them up. Write down the total.

2. Did you pay taxes to your state on your house, cottage, auto, or boat? How much? Add them up. Write down the total.

3. Did you pay interest on your home? How much? Write down that number.

4. Did you make charitable contributions? How much? Add them up, and write down the total.

5. Do you have miscellaneous deductions such as union dues, uniform expenses, fees on a safe deposit box that holds investments? Did you drive to get to your volunteer work? Fourteen cents per mile, both ways? Did you entertain in your home for

the benefit of a charity? What did you spend? Add it up and write it down.

You now have five numbers. Add them together. Is the number larger than last year's standard deduction? If not, you did the right thing by taking the standard deduction. If it is, you made a mistake; you should have filed the long form with Schedule A.

However, mistakes can be corrected. I am not talking about being wiser for next year. I am talking about correcting last year's mistake by filling out an amended income tax return. You already have done the work! Just transfer last year's information *plus* Schedule A to an amended income tax form.

Do not panic. Your librarian will help you. Fill it out. Put a stamp on it. Mail it.

Do not panic. You will not get audited. Okay, there is a slim possibility that you might get audited. So what? You have your records. You did not fudge even a little bit. You have absolutely nothing to worry about. You can look your God and the IRS in the eye. Now *that* is integrity!

Soon you will get a refund. I do not care if the refund is small or large. Your Net Wealth does not care if the refund is small or large. It will be glad for the extra weight.

Rest. Take a breather. Do not spend money in celebration of your victory. Dance a little dance, and report the win to your spouse. If she or he does not dance with you, she or he does not understand how the Not Wealth/Net Wealth Scale works. Help your spouse.

Enough rest. Back to making things easier and forcing the government to give you what you deserve while you give it what it deserves.

Two Incomes

We discovered earlier that in CMC families the second wage earner bears a disproportionate amount of income tax. We also discovered that the best way to build Net Wealth is not by adding a second income but by plugging leaks caused by not paying attention. (Remember the caveat: In some cases it may make emotional sense for a spouse to take a job outside the home.)

YOUR 401(K)

Let's say that you are gainfully and legally employed. (We are not going to quibble over whether attorneys fit that description.) Let's also say that you want to build your Net Wealth. Is it possible that the IRS could help us put more dollars on the *Own* side of the scale? You bet. Will they do it happily? If they smile, it will be a forced smile.

First, if you're married, talk to your spouse. Get him or her on board. Let your spouse know what is going down. Work through the excitement, fears, boredom, yawns, and so on.

Talk to your friendly payroll department. You are going to inquire about a 401(k) plan. Do not worry that you do not understand the 401(k). It is legal. You probably do not understand the computer that makes your car run, but you drive it anyway.

Essentially, the 401(k) plan is a vehicle to help you build a tax-deferred (not tax-free) retirement bonanza. By putting $100 of tax-deferred dollars into the plan every month, you will not have to pay *current* income taxes on it. This means your paycheck will not take a tax hit on this $100. Starting at 70.5 years of age, you must withdraw certain percentages from the account and pay tax on that amount. But in the meantime you earn compound interest on the whole $100 taco instead of a tax-bitten taco.

Does your company have a 401(k)? Good. (If the answer is no, ask why not? Do not let them intimidate you. Smile. Tell them you do not understand. What provision are they making for their employees' retirement years? No, Social Security is not enough. Smile. Thank them. When the job market gets better, move on.)

Anyway, back to the good companies. Ask for the proper forms to fill out. Fill them out properly. As you are doing that, inquire if the company matches a certain percentage of the employee's contributions. They do? Good. (If the answer is no, ask why not? Smile. You know the drill. If their answer is something like, "That idea has as much chance around here as a snowball enjoying Kansas City in July," smile. Thank them. When the job market...)

What percentage will the company match? Four percent? Wonderful. Put in a minimum of 4 percent of your salary into your 401(k) plan. You will get a 100 percent return on your investment, an immediate "sure-thing" return. As you know, in the investment world, there is no such thing as a sure-thing return. But there is in the 401(k) world if your company matches a portion of your contribution.

The same goes for IRAs, Roth IRAs, 403(b) accounts, and so on. It is not hard to read the material during one or two (or even three) Magic 80 sessions.

Does this not excite you? It should. Instead of our theme of "More life; less money," this time we have "More life, more money." It can hardly get better than that.

You have now done several things:
- added a lot of weight to the *Own* side of the scale,
- lessened the weight of the *Owe* side of the scale,
- received a 100 percent *immediate* return on your investment,
- lowered your taxes by saving in a tax-deferred plan,
- not lowered your paycheck nearly as much as you think, and
- had a victory.

If you are the RCEO in your home, but your spousal unit is the one whose company has a 401(k) program and he or she is too "tired" (read: confused) to activate that program, get the information and hand it to him or her. Draw an x by each place your spouse's signature is required. If you had to do this much, do not trust your spouse to get the forms into the proper hands. Take them yourself. And work harder at getting on the same page with your spouse. Your relationship isn't what it could be.

Now do not tell me that you can't afford to contribute to a 401(k) because you need every dime just to live. Okay, but I asked you not to tell me.

Go back to earlier sections of this book. Memorize them. Practice them for three months. If there is still a problem, call me. If you activate the plan, there will not be a problem unless you run into accident, illness, or disaster.

One section of the freeway to wealth is paved by not paying taxes that you do not have to pay.

STEPS TOWARD SHREWD

- Normal people can prepare their own taxes.
- It is *not* shrewd to shortchange the government.
- It *is* shrewd to stop paying the government more than you owe.
- Learn the forms; it is expensive to be naive.
- Itemize your deductions.
- Start working on taxes the November before they are due.
- Participate in any tax-deferred retirement plan that is available to you.

18

100 Days to Shrewd

I f you are a nonshrewd person, glued to Devastating and Decent Debt, living more in Not Wealth than in Net Wealth, what are you waiting for? Now is the time to turn things around, to move into the world of shrewd. Drastic situations call for drastic actions. That is why we are entering into a 100-day project to turn our lives around. We call it *100 Days to Shrewd*. You can do it.

I promise that you will not have to give up anything. That promise will hold as long as you follow the principles presented in this book. You will be adding so many neat things to your life (like visual evidence of moving from Not Wealth to Net Wealth) that you will not miss former patterns. Your experiences will not be grim loss. More life, less cost is our goal. New patterns are the answer. You will be different. The first difference will be in what you do, and the second difference will be in what you believe about money and how it affects you. You are at the point of mastering your money and making it serve you.

It is my assertion that a little bit of intentional poverty is good for everyone. Intentional poverty is chosen poverty. Long-term, forced poverty is not good for anyone…except the beautiful people, of course. Forced poverty is not fun. Intentional, chosen poverty can be fun.

You will need 100 days to accomplish this goal. Why 100 days? In a study I just made up, I demonstrated that 100 days will give you enough time to start the project, make progress, run into obstacles, overcome the obstacles, and gain confidence to move forward. (I have chosen to name my study "Common Sense.") That cycle will repeat itself. At the end of

100 days you will see with new eyes. Now is the time for you to put away your financial thinking that says "I must have it all now," and put on a new way of creative thinking that says "I have more than enough right now."

THE FIRST FORTY DAYS

First step: For the first forty days, track your spending. (Refer back to the single and double tracking methods in chapter 7. Remember, no shame, no blame.) If you're married, get on the same page with your spouse. Discover the James Bond or Sherlock Holmes within you. Become a spy and a sleuth; analyze the data you have gathered. Did you get full value (read: enjoyment) for each expenditure? If not, cut these costs or minimize them! You will be getting ideas on how to increase the Life Index and decrease the Cost Index. You will be working on how to explain to your family that money and fun are not locked together at the hip. Have you done a List of Favorites? Get it done; you will need it. (See chapter 5.)

THE DRACONIAN ADVENTURE

For the next thirty days, you will be experiencing *The Draconian Adventure.* This will give you an achievable goal that will jump-start you in the right direction. Stop spending…for thirty days. Do what you have to do and pay the bills you have to pay. Love life. Pretend you just lost your job; pretend that you are in an economic depression; pretend that I am coming to visit you. Do everything to eliminate debt and buy *nothing* for yourself. For thirty days. Work hard at increasing the Life Index. How many things on the List of Favorites are free? Major in these. (Go to appendix A for starters.)

You will be choosing poverty for one month. That means you will spend no money. Certainly you have bills. Pay them. But no money for nonessentials. And the barest of bones for food. Live out of the back of

The Top Ten Reasons to Intentionalize Poverty

1. Taking action will show the stuff of which you and your family are made.
2. It will help you and your family identify with most of the world.
3. You will discover resources you had forgotten about.
4. You will eat less and lose weight.
5. You will exercise more, get healthier, and have more fun.
6. You and your family will stop taking "common" things for granted.
7. You will be able to work on True Riches and will expose your kids to the lie that you can only have fun if you spend money.
8. You will use the surplus gained from your intentional poverty to reduce your debt or increase your assets.
9. You and your family will discover new ingenuity and enthusiasm.
10. You will toughen up.

your pantry and freezer. Oh, there is RICE-A-RONI—and popcorn—and SPAM. One month. Thirty days. You can do this!

No lattes! No eat-out lunches. No restaurant of *any* kind. Yes, McDonald's counts as a restaurant—sort of.

I see the plea for more money is still on the frontal lobe of your brain: You need more money.

I want to be gentle here: You boophead! You have all the money you need right now. And even if you don't think you do, there is an easy way to get more money through a little-known investment. You don't need money for this investment. You only need to choose between two things: (1) you can eliminate pain by postponing pleasure, or (2) you can invite pain by not postponing pleasure.

Perhaps a better way to say the same thing: You can change your pleasures for a short period of time. It will teach you that you are not stuck in life—old things can be put on the shelf, and new things can be learned and enjoyed.

Think of it this way: In the spring you put your wool sweaters away for the proper season and bring out the short sleeves. It would be very uncomfortable to wear heavy winter wool in July. Thus, you have learned you can postpone good things until the time is right to bring them back into your life.

For example: We will pretend you have a movie addiction as your major pleasure. Maybe the cause of this addiction is that you were almost in a movie at one time or a movie was made in your hometown or you just like the looks of some of the people. But if you have a movie addiction, you also have a loss of money addiction. Run the numbers: driving to and from the theater, tickets, nibbles in the theater, after-movie delights at the pie place, sitter, placating the kids, and a long-distance call to Mom telling her she has "got" to see this movie. *Ka-ching, ka-ching,* and *ka-ching* one more time. The numbers look like $38. Might be a "tetch" conservative, but let's err on that side. That way you will have greater trust in my words.

One of the disasters of financial books is that they usually make you feel guilty about going to movies. I will never do that; stupid perhaps, but never guilty. The idea of postponing pleasure suggests that you not spend $38 on movies *for a while.* Stop whining; it is not forever, only for a while. How long is a while? Until you are out of Devastating Debt and away from the pain that it brings. NO, NO, NO, and NO, it will not take you forever to get out of credit-card debt, only a while.

But you must stop throwing money at the wrong things. You must throw money at the right things until you are in a position to go back to your old, stupid habits. If you practice postponement of pleasure for a while and develop alternative pleasures, you might be able to have your cake and wolf it down too! In other words, your new pleasures may, over time, be able to fund your former pleasures. But it is just as possible that your old life will be dead; the new life is more fun and adventurous. Tough, that is you!

Instead of living high on the hog, you will choose to live low on the hog. You will be too busy to spend money. You will enjoy what you are doing. Enjoyment plus no money equals enjoying poverty.

This is a frontal attack on our financial blind spots. You know what a blind spot is when you drive: There is a vehicle we cannot see in either our rearview mirror or our sideview mirror. It is in our blind spot. If we move into that lane, we have, er, "difficulty."

We all have financial blind spots. All of us. But enjoying poverty will make the blind spots visible and take away their potential danger.

As I've mentioned, Margie and I have gone through times of financial poverty. We earned very little in comparison to like-educated people. We lived in affluent areas with all the pressures that come with those neighborhoods. We were in a ministry that believed the staff could live on faith, and the people from whom we bought services or supplies couldn't. There were many months when we received no income.

Since we didn't have much, we had to make a game of our spending. That meant plan, plan, and plan some more. We heated our home with wood. Yes, the winters in Grand Rapids, Michigan, were chilly, and they had a tendency to last a long time. But gas heat was an expense we could do without. So we did. The gas company came out to investigate whether we were bypassing the meter. We didn't even have the pilot light on in the furnace. But it was legal. While I was gathering the year's wood supply, I was not spending money.

Though all thumbs, I became adept at home maintenance and repair. My apologies to my wife and children for what they had to endure during that process. While I was repairing and maintaining, I was not spending money.

I found I enjoyed gardening, both flowers and vegetables. We cultivated over 1,000 square feet on our suburban lot. Our neighbors loved it when we came up with creative ideas, such as landscaping with fruit trees and bushes as well as sharing our produce. While I was doing something I enjoyed, I was not spending money. Most of our meals came out of that garden every August. We did not spend money.

Creative vacations and entertainment became the norm. If I had a business engagement, Margie and I tried to see how we could piggyback a vacation off of it. We limited our expenditure of money.

The library became a major budget enhancer. We did not spend money. Oops, I believe we had two or three fines for turning books in late.

Early in the lives of Matt and Jodi, Margie developed a great eye for bargains at garage sales. As the kids grew older, she switched to buying clothes on sale. We spent minimal money.

Margie learned to cut my hair. More money not spent.

We only had one car for nine years. We didn't spend money. But can you imagine the celebration when we could "afford" a second car?

We bought antique furniture and decorating items that appreciated in value. We did not feel deprived as we saw what people around us had. As a matter of fact, we felt sorry for neighbors who were financially rich, but truly poor.

Do you catch the theme? While engaged in productive home activity, we did not spend money. We saved money, in fact: after-tax money. The best kind.

Now meals are going to be the line of demarcation for most families. They will start to throw in the towel on the 30-day Draconian Plan *unless* their stomachs are okay. But remember Table Manner 4? Toughness. That's you, tough! How will you get tough? Learn something new. Like cooking.

Go to the library. Check out some cookbooks. Make sure they are not ones with printed recipes and no pictures. Make sure they are the ones with beautiful color pictures. Next, look at what you have in the house. Look in the back of your pantry. You will now use all those things you bought on impulse and have pushed out of sight. Look in the freezer. What do you have?

You have to think and you have to plan. But you can do it. Who says it is wrong to have a couple of peanut butter sandwiches with a glass of milk for dinner? Who says that scrambled eggs and blueberry muffins do not count as a meal? Who says that if you give your family rice and beans, you are mean?

We have lived that way. Draconian is a great way to catch a dose of reality *and* pay down your debt, or save for a goal, or help the likes of Compassion International, or your church's deacon fund. In addition, it gives you an idea of how people in other parts of the world live.

Puzzles, board games, hikes, the library are all assets you have on hand. The key is leadership in the family. If you and your spousal unit are on the same page, your attitudes will carry the day. Have you ever had a family talent show?

Okay, thirty days is up. You did it! I knew you could. Now you get to graduate to the next level.

THE SPARTAN LIFESTYLE

For the next thirty days, you will come to know the *Spartan Lifestyle.* You will have more leeway in your spending but will still keep away from old destructive patterns. No luxuries and no entertainment. Pretend that you have a new job but cannot start for thirty days. On day thirty, give your family a treat. Pay with cash.

Your shrewdness will be off to a good start as firmly planted ongoing support principles have become a natural part of your life.

You did it again! I knew you could.

Shrewd, that is now you. After forty days of same-page understanding and sixty days of the Draconian Adventure and the Spartan Lifestyle, you will have a new outlook on life. You will understand your spending, you will have paid down debts, you will have had more fun, and life will be richer. Money will not have nearly the hold on you that it did just a few weeks ago.

How will you reward your family? That is up to you and your spousal unit. Pay cash.

Graduation! After you have completed your 100 days of shrewd living, please write to me at www.shrewdchristian.com, tell me your story, and I will send you a splendid diploma celebrating your feat.

STEPS TOWARD SHREWD

- Track your expenses for forty days.
- Live the Draconian Adventure for thirty days: Spend nothing!
- Live the Spartan Lifestyle for thirty days: Begin to spend again, but no luxuries.
- Graduate to shrewdness! Congratulations!

Conclusion

We will become truly rich only if our relationships grow. One could say that growth is the only evidence of life. This is true in terms of our faith and how our faith is growing in terms of daily living. Continual growth in marriage is just as true. Growth means getting on the same page and practicing Win/Win or No Deal. If we are growing toward being truly rich, we are winning the financial war. If our relationships are dull, dim, or dumb (as in silent), it is time for a relational makeover. ASAP.

We will become financially wealthy only if we pay attention to the Little Things (done Excellently, of course) over time and Apply them Appropriately. We must pay attention and guard the financial back door at all times. If you are married, both you and your spouse need to be on the same page.

The truly rich/financially wealthy idea is a guide toward appropriate discipleship. How we use our money is a good indicator of what we really believe about Jesus. If we ignore money or stop at money, the chances of being a poor disciple loom large. Without going *through* money and getting past it, we will be slaves to that which is the enemy of Jesus. If we do not fight out of the cocoon of money, we will not develop the spiritual musculoskeletal system so that we are tough enough to be called "disciple."

Once we are past money, we will be really free. That kind of freedom means we can be wild in our commitment: go anywhere and do anything to which the Lord of the universe calls us.

The greatest motivator for action is pain. Until it hurts intensely and over a period of time, we will not see the dentist, the doctor, the chiropractor, or the podiatrist. When we finally see her, we are relieved because she can do something about our pain—and we might be distressed that we didn't do something earlier.

Pain is also a motivator in the financial world. Until we are in severe fiscal pain, we will probably continue to deny and ignore it. As the pain becomes more acute, we realize we must get help. That help is the key to our transformation. The help identifies the problem. At first, it is agonizing; the pain of correct diagnosis is now added to the pain previously experienced. The pain has been multiplied; things are looking grim. What good could possibly come out of all this pain and darkness?

Let me give you an example. As I was writing this book, I noticed that my hands were not working correctly. I would often look at what I had typed and discover that many words began with the letter *d*. Unfortunately, the *d* did not belong. I then noticed my hands were sore after working at the computer. Finally, I noticed I was losing strength. My middle fingers were so painful that I could not recruit them when I was lifting things. The straw that broke the back of my physician-resistance was the realization that I could no longer grip a golf club!

Dr. Weber at first thought my pain was arthritis in my neck (you know, all those little hand nerves pass through the neck). She gave me some superstrength over-the-counter pain medication and said, "Get used to it. Welcome to the aging process." One month later I took my aging body back to her office and said, "I do not want to get used to the pain." She is a good physician. She said, "It is time to see a hand specialist."

Dr. Steve Topper looked at my hands, tapped a few places, asked questions, and finally said, "Carpal tunnel syndrome—or a nerve disease." Nerve disease? That got my attention. Dr. Topper said, "Not to worry, I will send you to a specialist for a nerve test." Little did I know what a nerve test meant. Sometimes it is good to be dumb.

I will not tell you the name of the doctor who performed this barbaric form of diagnosis. I was concerned as I looked at the devices that he was going to use. But shoot, I am an adult male and I can handle stuff. (As the doctor walked in, I noticed a black hood over his head. Too late.)

The test consisted of electric shocks applied to fifty points (okay, eight, but it felt like fifty) on my hands and arms. Whew, finally, it was over. I started to sit up and a smile crossed his face as he said, "We are not finished yet." Uh oh.

Shocks were bad, but not nearly as bad as pins being stuck where the shocks had been applied. When he stuck the pin into the base of my right thumb, I actually levitated six inches off the table. I was so exhausted by the experience that I drove straight to Starbucks and chugged down a caffeinated drink.

Dr. Torture did give me good news: no nerve disease, it was carpal tunnel syndrome. I will have surgery after the book is finished. I believe in my heart of hearts the surgery will be less painful than the diagnostic procedure; even if they do it without anesthesia.

The best news is that within six weeks, my hands will be back to normal. I can see the future, and it is pain free.

I see your relational and financial future. It is pain free. However, (there is that word again) you might have to engage in diagnostic pain, surgical pain, and recuperation pain to get there. The goal is to get past the pain caused by money mastering us, to freedom of pain caused by money serving us.

How? One step at time. In the words of Isaiah: "They will walk and not be faint" (Isaiah 40:31). You can do it!

Ideas for Frugal Fun

It is entirely possible to have more fun with a $4 Frisbee than a $40,000 boat. If you are living in the kingdom of Right Relationships, everything and anything can be fun most of the time. If you are not on the same page with your spouse in a Right Relationship, then nothing can be fun. But spending money can be a distraction from the pain of not being on the same page or in a Right Relationship. Work on it. Shrewd Christians are tough!

Here are forty ways to increase the Life Index and reduce the Cost Index:

1. Learn something new: a game, a skill, something that appeals to your mate, your friend, or your child. Experiment.
2. Renew acquaintances with things you used to enjoy (e.g., ballet, piano, softball, kite flying, bird-watching).
3. Dust off your Bible. Read it.
4. Clean, organize, and eliminate. Donate or have a garage sale.
5. Plan a vacation at home. The goal: Make it more fun than any other vacation you have ever taken.
6. Get a "new" car. Spend one auto day doing the interior (e.g., carpets, seats, dash, console, and inside of windows) and exterior (e.g., wash job, tires, and wax job). This strategy works very well for helping you hold on to your car while you save for another one.
7. Visit the library. (You do have a library card, correct?) Renew your relationship with the free advice and resources (e.g., videos, DVDs, magazines, Internet access, computer courses).

8. Have a handicapped day. To learn about the difficulties of the disabled, pretend to be disabled for a day. For example, put someone's arm in a sling; gently tie your children's legs together, or let someone put a blindfold around your eyes. Talk about the experiences.

9. The one-month cook day. Plan, plan, plan. Cook, cook, cook. Spend one Saturday cooking. Make huge meals, divide them into meal-size portions, and freeze them. Make all lunches for the coming week.

10. Teach your kids to do things: operate the washer and dryer, maneuver the vacuum cleaner, locate the garbage can. If they are old enough, they can graduate to the lawn mower.

11. Eat breakfast for dinner. Shoot, eat ice cream for dinner!

12. Have a neighborhood potluck or progressive dinner.

13. Explore your park system.

14. Work a day with Habitat for Humanity.

15. Visit museums and arboretums.

16. Move the television to the basement.

17. Explore local hiking trails.

18. Go for a family swim.

19. Visit the zoo. Kids like zoos. (Find a coupon.)

20. Build a campfire (in a safe and legal spot!) and roast bratwurst and s'mores.

21. Play foursquare on your driveway. Our friends The Gum Gang (Jim, five boys, and poor Lee) love to play this game. Even the youngest arrives at the champion's square.

22. Stay up late on a Friday night. Sleep late on Saturday morning. Have breakfast for lunch.

23. Ride bicycles or go sledding (use a cardboard box with the end turned up).

24. If you live in a safe neighborhood, go for a midnight stroll in the moonlight.

25. Do puzzles. (My editor buys puzzles at garage sales. She and her husband do them for fun. And they are young!)

26. Play chess, Monopoly, checkers.

27. Teach your kids to cook. Shoot, teach your spouse to cook.

28. Go on picnics—summer, fall, winter, spring.

29. Take a break from the indoor exercise equipment and exercise outdoors for a change—soccer, kickball, softball, basketball.

30. Garden—the whole enchilada!

31. Cut your own Christmas tree.

32. Get to know your neighbors.

33. Build a snowman or have a neighborhood snowball fight.

34. Learn to laugh more—it goes hand in hand with refusing to take yourself seriously.

35. Donate items to organizations that feed and clothe the poor—it goes hand in hand with taking the Lord seriously.

36. Volunteer to serve meals to the homeless on Thanksgiving—or anytime.

37. Have friends over for dinner, but serve what you would serve your family at a typical meal (e.g., rice and beans, pizza, spaghetti). (Let them know what you will be serving.)

38. Write thank-yous to your parents, spouse, children, pastors, teachers, and others.

39. Work hard at forgiving your enemies.

40. Work hard at forgiving yourself.

What are some of the things *you're* doing to have more fun with less money? You will come up with fantastic ideas that will kill four birds with half a stone. The confidence, excitement, and sense of accomplishment will allow you to tackle other areas. Could you give up your parking garage and walk an extra two blocks? (Shoot, you would kill two birds with one little stone on that baby.) Could you take the stroller and walk to the grocery store and only buy exactly what you need? (Another two birds have fallen.)

Be creative. Contact me at www.shrewdchristian.com and let me know what you come up with. Only do not send me ideas that you *plan* to do. Send me ideas that you have *already* done and have seen work. Good ideas stand the test of time and reality.

For Emergencies and Disasters Only

I f this section is the one that drew your immediate attention, it is likely that you are staring at a significant loss of income. Thus, the information in this book is no longer a "nice" exercise, but a means toward survival. This chapter could be the start of that survival.

What do you do now? This book cannot provide the "perfect" recipe for you. However, based on working with many people who have experienced a loss of income, I have a few suggestions that could provide initial direction, which you can refine to fit your needs.

A few years ago I ran across a great book titled *Tough Times Don't Last, but Tough People Do.* Toughness is a condition for becoming a Shrewd Christian. This is an abbreviated starter kit if you find yourself in an extreme situation.

1. Most important: Do not panic. Yet. I will tell you when it is time to panic. Just wait.

2. If you were fired, get the facts as to why you were terminated. Your fault? How so? Their fault? The economy's fault? Be kind to the person who fired you. This will help you in your next job.

3. If you lost your job for any reason other than cause, what benefits do you get: severance, vacation, health? Check to see that your company's analysis matches yours.

4. You must conserve your resources. The first resource is your energy. Recognize that forced separation from work or a spouse or a business is a death experience. As with physical death, you will go through huge mood swings: anger, relief, fear, joy,

numbness, excitement, shock, and so on. Let the emotions out in an appropriate manner. Stay as calm as you can. It is not time to panic.

5. It *is* time to inventory what can aid you in this time of stress.
   - Do you have a support group? Let them know and have them pray. Let your church know and have them pray.
   - Look at what money you have on hand. How much do you have in a savings account, checking account, cash? Does anyone owe you money that you could collect? Is any cash coming your way? How long can you meet expenses with the money on hand?
   - What is your living situation like? If life has been too hectic and you have not been shopping with SOE (Save on Everything) in mind, you could be a little lean. What do you have in your cupboards, refrigerator, freezer, closets, garage, and basement that could help? These are assets that are consumable or sellable. It is not time to panic.
   - What bills are due this month as well as during the next six months?
   - What expenditures must be made in the next month or you or yours will die, literally?
   - Look carefully at all the information listed on the asset paper. Study it.

6. Now it is time to panic. But be sure to do it correctly. Following are the Atkinson's Rules of Panic.
   - You are allowed any and all feelings and words. NO holds barred! You are going to have the greatest panic session ever known to humankind.
   - You will remember every unfairness, injustice, frustration, and hurt. You will have a projectile vomiting of fear, worry, guilt, and anxiety. Doesn't that sound like fun?

- Therefore, you will do this in a place where no one else can *hear* you. That way you will be sure to let it *all* happen.
- You will do this for no more than ten minutes. Bring an accurate watch.
- You will do it on a Tuesday or a Thursday.
- You will do it between 6:00 a.m. and 6:30 a.m.
- You will do it only once. Make it a good one.
- You may *not* alter any of the above rules: ten minutes, one time.
- You are finished with panic.
- Let's get on with your life.

7. You can make it on what you have in your possession. For a long time. Much longer than you think. Remember, this is an emergency, and a greater disaster is looming if you do not make adjustments.

   - Bring your family up to speed. If your parents and in-laws are supportive people, bring them up to speed. If either set is toxic, ignore them for the time being. There is only so much energy within you; don't waste it on people who will drag you down. You can deal with them later.
   - If your kids are old enough to receive money (i.e., they receive an allowance or they ask for money), include them in the session. Everyone must see reality. Clearly. Ask for their cooperation, help, and prayer.
   - You are now on a money diet. You don't realize you are tough, but you are. You can do this!

8. You will eat and drink only what you have on hand until it is all gone. Remember, water is good for you.

9. You will plan each and every errand to be efficient and effective for your life—as well as your vehicle.

10. Your entertainment will be at home with your family. Board games and such. No rental movies—to say nothing of actual movies.

11. Stay away from temptation. Do not let the siren song of the mall lure you into its grasp. Those who run the mall are professionals at getting people like you into their grasp. "Oh, you lost your job? Well, let's help you look your best for that job interview! This suit is 50 percent off today! Aren't you the lucky one.… You do have a credit card, don't you?"

12. Now you are in a position to look for a new career. You are in charge of your life and talents, values and interests. Make sure that your new job is one that fits.

13. Consider that you may have to take a Plan-B job temporarily until your Plan-A job comes along. Just don't settle for Plan B and get too comfortable.

14. What do you say to your family and friends who expect you to be a whining wimp or wimpette? "Well, I admit, I was panicked for a little while. But I got over that. I did an inventory of our assets, and we are okay for a while. I do not have to rush into anything. Now I am working a strategy to find a job that fits me and allows me to make a contribution. A wise man told me that too many people take what is available when they are vulnerable. I don't want to be in that place. To get to my 'A' job, I may have to get some more education or take a temporary 'B' job. Thanks for asking."

15. Get an assessment of your strengths. (The IDAK Career Match is the best thing on the market. This is a process that helps you understand what you can do. Most career testing uses personality tests to tell you what you are like. You can find out more by visiting the IDAK Group Web site at www.idakgroup.com.)

16. Match your strengths to specific jobs. (Once again, the IDAK Career Match will help here.)

17. Apply due diligence. Find men and women who have jobs you might be interested in pursuing. Visit them at their offices and find out about their day-to-day job responsibilities. That kind of interview will help you decide on a career target.

18. Once you know what you want to do, you can look for an organization that needs that job done. Or you can prepare to become trained, educated, or certified for that job.

The important thing is to recognize the valuable resources you already possess, to maximize them, and to increase your efficiency, effectiveness, and productivity.

If you choose to intentionally downsize your lifestyle, you will recognize that the very best things are already in your possession: faith, health, family, friends, and new self-esteem. The self-esteem comes from staring at the tiger that wants to devour you, spitting in its eye, and tearing off its head. No wimpy Shrewd Christian. Tough, that's you.

Another benefit: In as little as three weeks, your family and friends will notice a new you. You have shaped the finances and the home into a fort that can withstand almost every onslaught. You will have reshaped your outsides and dropped a few pounds. The true truth is that you will have developed a can-do attitude.

Now that you have a specific idea of how this is working, turn to the chapter titled "100 Days to Shrewd." Practice what it preaches. And follow the principles in the rest of this book.

You are not alone. Thousands upon thousands of people have lost their jobs in the last few years. Do not give up. Do not settle for second best. Stay the course!

NOTES

Chapter 3

1. From Robert D. Manning, *Credit Card Nation: The Consequences of America's Addiction to Credit* (New York: Basic Books, 2001).
2. From a sales presentation prepared by Brett Posten and Robert Ten-Eyck in September 2002. Used by permission.

Chapter 4

1. From Thomas J. Stanley, *The Millionaire Mind* (Kansas City, Mo.: Andrews McMeel, 2001).
2. To learn more about millionaires, read Thomas J. Stanley and William D. Danko's excellent book, *The Millionaire Next Door* (New York: Simon & Schuster, 1998).
3. From Stanley and Danko, *The Millionaire Next Door,* and Thomas J. Stanley, *The Millionaire Mind.*

Chapter 5

1. From Stephen R. Covey, *The 7 Habits of Highly Effective People* (New York: Simon & Schuster, 1989).

Chapter 6

1. AARP, "A Report to the Nation on Economic Security: Executive Summary." Found at www.aarp.org.

Chapter 7

1. From Joe Dominguez and Vicki Robin, *Your Money or Your Life: Transforming Your Relationship with Money and Achieving Financial Independence* (New York: Penguin, 1999).

Chapter 8

1. Gordon MacDonald, *Secrets of the Generous Life* (Wheaton, Ill.: Tyndale, 2002), v.

2. From Barna Research Online, "Stewardship," 23 September 2003. Found at www.barna.org.

3. Richard Foster, *Money, Sex, and Power* (San Francisco: HarperSan-Francisco, 1985), 71.

Chapter 9

1. "Sixteen Tons," original lyrics by George Davis, copyright © 1947 by Merle Travis.

2. From Manning, *Credit Card Nation.*

3. From Manning, *Credit Card Nation.*

Chapter 10

1. To learn more about the economically productive household (EPH), read *The Millionaire Next Door.*

2. From Stanley and Danko, *The Millionaire Next Door,* 32.

3. Stanley and Danko, *The Millionaire Next Door,* 11, 31.

4. From Teri Agins, "Cheapskate Chic," *Wall Street Journal,* 15 October 2001.

Chapter 11

1. From the U.S. Department of Labor Bureau of Labor Statistics, "National Compensation Survey of Occupational Wages in the United States in July 2002." Found at www.bls.gov.

2. Dominguez and Robin, *Your Money or Your Life,* 3.

3. The "Lucky Seven" are Alaska, Florida, Nevada, South Dakota, Texas, Washington, and Wyoming. New Hampshire and Tennessee also do not have personal income tax, but they do tax interest and dividend income.

Chapter 12

1. From Stanley and Danko, *The Millionaire Next Door,* 37.

Chapter 17

1. Stuart Kessler, "8 Tips to Reduce Your Tax Bite," *AARP Bulletin,* February 2003. Found at www.aarp.org.

ABOUT THE AUTHOR

NEIL ATKINSON is not a financial expert, but he has learned what it means to become and remain truly wealthy. A graduate of Hope College and Fuller Seminary, Neil worked with Young Life for thirty-two years in a variety of leadership positions. There he discovered how to thrive, not just survive, on a meager ministry salary. In 1996 Neil founded Next! Leadership Development, helping people pursue God's calling on their lives. Neil and his wife, Margie, live in Colorado Springs. They have two grown children and one granddaughter.

If you would like to write to Neil with questions, please visit www.shrewdchristian.com.